Get INVOLVED!

American Edition

1

Student's Book

with Digital Student's Book

Gill Holley Kate Pickering

Get INVOLVED! American Edition

Collaborative projects

Collaborate with your classmates to develop your problem-solving skills in the WDYT? projects. Become an expert on a topic and get involved with others in your class.

WDYT?
(What do you think?)

Real-world content

Learn about culture while you learn English. *Get Involved! American Edition* is full of real-world content, so go online and learn more about the people, events and places in the book.

Super skills

Get Involved! American Edition helps develop your critical thinking, collaboration, creativity and communication skills, which are essential for life in the 21st century.

COLLABORATION **CRITICAL THINKING**

COMMUNICATION **CREATIVITY**

Building skills for the real world

Social and emotional learning

Get Involved! American Edition helps you develop strategies to deal with social situations and gives you the vocabulary you need to discuss emotions that you or others experience.

Ways to be polite

- Be friendly. Look at people and 1 __________ when you talk to them.

Media-rich content

Get Involved! American Edition videos help you with critical thinking, communication and project presentations and improve your video literacy skills. Access On-the-Go Practice on your phone through the Macmillan Student's App and improve your English with gamified content.

Inclusive classroom

Show your strengths and talents by putting your investigative skills and logic to the test with *Get Involved! American Edition* Brain teasers. Learn at your own pace with reinforcement and challenge activities in the Grammar bootcamp and graded Workbook activities.

BRAIN TEASER

2nd letter	3rd letter	2nd letter	4th letter	1st letter
l				

Look at the clues and write the correct letter. Then order the letters to make something you can eat.

What's the secret word?

Grammar bootcamp

Unit 1

Simple present: affirmative and negative

1 Reinforcement Change affirmative to negative and negative to affirmative.

1 I take a shower before breakfast.

LISTENING	REAL-WORLD SPEAKING	WRITING	PRONUNCIATION	PROJECT
Grammar: *be* (affirmative, negative and questions), possessive adjectives, possessive *'s* and *s'*, *have got*, *can* for ability				
A conversation British and Finnish teenagers comparing their schools **Subskill:** Identifying the type of listening	Working together to check answers	**A blog post** **Subskill:** Capital letters	Silent letters	Design a schedule for your ideal school. **Critical thinking** Making logical decisions
A radio interview with a hockey player **Subskill:** Listening for the general idea	Asking for information	**Informal messages** **Subskill:** and, or and but	*do you* /djʊ/	Do a survey about how students in the class spend their free time. **Collaboration** Planning and task management
A live report about No Uniform Day **Subskill:** Listening to questions and answers	Shopping for clothes	**Photo descriptions** **Subskill:** because and so	/n/ and /ŋ/	Make a mini-book about traditional clothes. **Creativity** Using your imagination and thinking of original ideas
Instructions for an adventure vacation in Yosemite **Subskill:** Using pictures to help you understand	Making and responding to suggestions	**Instructions** **Subskill:** too and also	*can*	Make a video giving weather advice to visitors to your country. **Communication** Active listening
An informal conversation about a visit to Buenos Aires **Subskill:** Predicting vocabulary	Asking for directions	**A description of a place** **Subskill:** Adjectives	/i/ and /ɪ/	Make a map showing useful places for young people moving to live in your town. **Critical thinking** Considering the needs of other people
A podcast about a teen entrepreneur **Subskill:** Identifying which statements are true or false	Showing interest	**An email** **Subskill:** Sequencing words	Simple past endings /d/ /t/ /ɪd/	Prepare a poster about endangered animals to raise awareness and help to protect them. **Collaboration** Listening to other people's opinions
A podcast about two talented teens **Subskill:** Listening for numbers	Giving opinions	**A biography** **Subskill:** Writing in paragraphs	Schwa /ə/	Make a digital presentation about a hero from the past. **Creativity** Using feedback to improve your work
Phone conversations and messages about vacation plans **Subskill:** Listening for feelings	Making arrangements	**Invitations** **Subskill:** Apostrophes	*will*	Create a three-day vacation plan for you and your friends. **Communication** Communicating clearly
Listening: review of subskills		**Speaking:** review of Key phrases		**Writing:** review of subskills

Project planner p130 Irregular verbs p134

STARTER What do you know?

All around the world

Vocabulary: countries and nationalities

1 Complete the tables.

Country	Nationality
Australia	1
2	Brazilian
Canada	3
4	Chinese
France	5
6	Irish
7	Japanese

Country	Nationality
8	Mexican
Morocco	9
10	Nigerian
Spain	11
12	Turkish
the UK	13
14	American

2 1 Listen and check. Identify the stressed syllable.

Australia – Australian

3 Work in pairs. Complete the quiz with countries in exercise 1. You have three minutes!

Grammar: *be* (affirmative, negative and *Yes/No* questions)

4 Complete the table with *is*, *isn't*, *are* and *aren't*.

Affirmative	
I'm	American.
You/We/They 1 ________	
He/She/It 2 ________	
Negative	
I'm not	French.
You/We/They 3 ________	
He/She/It 4 ________	

5 Write affirmative or negative sentences. Add capital letters.

1 he / from  (+) *He's from Japan.*
2 she /  (–) *She isn't Irish.*
3 we / from  (+) ________
4 it /  (–) ________
5 I /  (+) ________
6 you / from  (–) ________

THE BIG WORLD QUIZ

1 Name three countries where people speak English.

2 Tokyo is the capital city of …

3 Name three countries in Europe.

4 Name two countries where people speak Spanish.

5 Say five countries with the letter 'r' in their names.

6 Name two countries in Africa.

Reinforcement and Challenge | Grammar bootcamp p116

6 **Read the examples and circle the correct option to complete the rules.**

> **Are you** Spanish? — No, **I'm not.**
> **Are you** Mexican? — Yes, **I am.**

1 For *Yes/No* questions, *be* comes **first/second**.
2 For short answers in the affirmative, **use/ don't use** contractions.
3 For short answers in the negative, **use/don't use** contractions.

7 **Match questions 1–5 with answers a–e.**

1	Is she a teacher?	a	No, it isn't.
2	Are we on exercise 4?	b	Yes, she is.
3	Are they your pens?	c	No, they aren't.
4	Is it the correct answer?	d	Yes, you are.
5	Am I in the right classroom?	e	No, we aren't.

Are you new here?

Vocabulary: in the classroom

1 2 **Listen and write the letters. What words do you hear?**

2 **Complete the words with vowels to make classroom objects.**

1 CL __ CK
2 B __ __ K
3 P __ NC __ L
4 CH __ __ R
5 B __ __ RD
6 C __ MP __ T __ R
7 N __ T __ B __ __ K
8 SH __ RP __ N __ R
9 D __ CT __ __ N __ RY
10 W __ ND __ W

3 **Work in pairs. Point to something in the classroom and ask and answer the questions.**

What's this?

It's a notebook.

this/these, that/those

Ask *'What's **this**?'* (singular) and *'What are **these**?'* (plural) for things near you.
Ask *'What's **that**?'* (singular) and *'What are **those**?'* (plural) for things at a distance.

4 3 **Listen to the instructions and match them with pictures a–f.**

a	b	c	d	e	f
	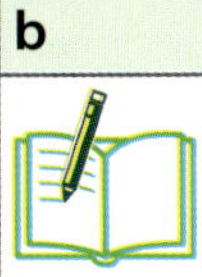		They *are* French.		He's from France.

5 4 **Listen and match conversations 1–4 with pictures A–D.**

A __

B __

C __

D __

Grammar: *be* (*Wh-* questions)

6 **Read the examples and circle the correct option in the rule.**

> **What's** this? — **It's** a pen.
> **What are** those? — **They're** my books.

For *Wh-* questions, the verb comes **before/ after** the question word.

7 **Match the question words in the box with pictures 1–5.**

How old? What? When? Where? Who?

1	2	3	4	5

8 **Order the words to make questions.**

1 name / your / What's ?
2 you from / Where / are ?
3 are / How old / you ?
4 favorite sport / What's / your ?
5 your / favorite singer / Who's ?

9 **Work in pairs. Ask and answer the questions in exercise 8.**

Families – big and small

Vocabulary: family

1 **Copy and complete the table with the family words in the box.**

aunt ~~brother~~ cousin daughter father grandfather grandmother mother nephew niece parent sister son uncle

Male	Female	Both
brother		

2 **Write the family member.**

1 Your mother's brother *uncle*
2 Your father's mother ________
3 Your sister's son ________
4 Your mother's daughter ________
5 Your aunt's son ________

mother and father = parents
son and daughter = children

3 **Work in pairs. Describe the families in the photos.**

I think this is the mother.

Or maybe they're three sisters ...

A

B

C

D

4 **Match family descriptions 1–3 with photos A–D in exercise 3. There is one photo you don't need.**

Families around the world

Some of our readers tell us about their families.

1 I live with my family in New York. My dad's from India, and my aunts, uncles and cousins all live there. My dad's name is Samar and he's 45 years old. My mom's 39. Her name is Liz. I've got two sisters. __

2 I've got three sisters. My older sister's married and she's got a son and a daughter. My nephew's name is Jia and my niece is named Fin. My grandmother lives with us. I've got six cousins. __

3 I live with my mom and my sister. We're a small family, but we're close to our neighbors. They're named Mr. and Mrs. Evans and their sons' names are Caleb and Damien. They're like brothers to me. __

5 **Find 12 family members in the descriptions.**

Grammar: possessive adjectives

6 **Read the example. Copy and complete the table with the possessive adjectives in the box.**

My mom's 39. **Her** name is Liz.

his its our their your

Subject pronouns	I	you	he	she	it	we	they
Possessive adjectives	*my*	1	2	*her*	3	4	5

7 **Complete the sentences with possessive adjectives.**

1 My grandfather is 70 years old. ________ name's Frank.
2 My cousins live with ________ parents in the USA.
3 We've got a big yard, but ________ house is small.
4 My sister lives with ________ husband and two children.
5 What about you? Is ________ family big or small?

Reinforcement and Challenge Grammar bootcamp p116

Grammar: possessive *'s* and *s'*

My nephew**'s** name is Jia. (singular noun + **'s**)
Their sons**'** names are Caleb and Damien. (plural noun ending in *s* + **'**)

8 Add one apostrophe (') to each sentence.

1 My dads family is in India.
2 My grandparents house is in Chennai.
3 I see my cousins at my uncles house.
4 My cousins names are Ajay and Hari.

Who is it?

Vocabulary: describing people

1 Find the people in the picture.

1 He's got black hair and a mustache. He wears glasses. He hasn't got a beard.
2 She's got short blond hair and blue eyes.
3 He's got light hair. He hasn't got a beard.
4 She's tall. She's got short curly hair and glasses.

2 Complete the table with the words in exercise 1.

General description	Hair	Hair color	Eyes	Other
short	*long* *straight*	*brown* *gray*	*brown* *green*	*beard*

3 🔊 5 Listen and match the descriptions to the people in exercise 1.

Grammar: *have got*

4 Complete the table with *has*, *hasn't* or *haven't*.

	Affirmative	Negative
I/You/We/They	**have got** black hair.	1 _________ **got** blue eyes.
He/She/It	2 _________ **got** short hair.	3 _________ **got** glasses.

5 Complete the sentences with the correct form of *have got*.

1 He _________ a beard and glasses. (+)
2 They _________ any children. (-)
3 I _________ a cat named Sam. (+)
4 We _________ any cousins. (-)
5 She _________ any brothers or sisters. (-)

6 Complete the table with *has*, *hasn't*, *have* or *haven't*.

Questions	Short answers
Have you **got** curly hair?	Yes, I **have**./No, I **1** _________
2 _________ he **got** a beard?	Yes, he **has**./No, he **3** _________
Have they **got** blue eyes?	Yes, they **4** _________ /No, they **haven't**.

7 Write questions with *have got*.

1 you / any brothers or sisters ?
2 your dad / a beard ?
3 your mom / long hair ?
4 your parents / any brothers or sisters ?
5 you / a lot of cousins ?

8 Work in pairs. Ask and answer the questions in exercise 7. Then write a description of your partner's family.

Tania's got a big family. She's got two brothers ...

9 Read the text and answer the question.

BRAIN TEASER

Two parents have got six sons. Each son has got a sister.

How many people are there in the family?

What can you do?

Vocabulary: action verbs

1 **Match the words in the box with photos 1–10.**

cook dance draw play ride run
sing speak spell swim

1 ________

2 ________

3 ________

4 ________

5 ________ a bike

6 ________ the guitar

7 ________

8 ________ Chinese

9 ________

10 ________ fast

2 6 **Listen. What is the verb? Can the people do the action?**

1 *sing – yes*

Grammar: *can* for ability

3 **Complete the table with sentences a–d.**

a He can't spell.
b Can they cook?
c Yes, they can.
d She can swim.

Affirmative	Negative
I **can** draw. 1 ________ They **can** speak Chinese.	I **can't** sing. 2 ________ They **can't** speak French.
Questions	**Short answers**
Can you play the guitar? **Can** he sing? 3 ________	Yes, I **can**./No, I **can't**. Yes, he **can**./No, he **can't**. 4 ________ /No, they **can't**.

4 **Use the words to write questions (?) and affirmative (+) or negative (–) sentences.**

1 she / sing (+)
2 he / play the guitar (–)
3 she / speak Chinese (?)
4 he / swim (+)
5 they / spell (–)
6 you / dance (?)

5 **Work in pairs. Ask and answer questions about the activities in exercise 4. How many of your answers are the same?**

Can you sing?

No, I can't.

6 **Work in pairs. Test yourself!**

Test

What can you do in English?

Score ONE point for each thing you can do.

1 name six colors
2 write the names of ten animals
3 see three things that begin with the letter 'C'
4 count backwards from 20 to 1 (20, 19, 18, ...)
5 spell your teacher's name
6 say the days of the week

Reinforcement and Challenge Grammar bootcamp p117

What's in this book?

1 **Look through the Student's Book and answer the questions.**

1 Each unit has a **Quick review** page. Where?
2 How many **Projects** are there in the book?
3 Where is the **Irregular verbs** list?
4 Where is the **Graphic organizer?**

2 **There are lots of things to help you in the book. Find the answers to the questions.**

1 In **WDYT? (What Do You Think?)** you think about a big question at the start of the unit, and again at the end. Lots of things in the unit help you think about the topic. What's the question in Unit 2?
2 In **Research** boxes you go online to find out more about a topic. What information do you research in Unit 4?
3 In **Video skills** you learn to think critically about videos. What's the first question in Video skills in Unit 6?
4 In **Reading subskills** you learn how to be a more effective reader. What's the subskill in Unit 1?
5 In **Word work** you meet new vocabulary in context in the reading texts. What's the first word you study in Unit 7?
6 In **Critical thinking** you learn to think more carefully about ideas in a text. What's question number 3 in the Critical thinking activity in Unit 5?
7 In **Listening subskills** you learn how to be a more effective listener. What's the subskill in Unit 3?
8 In **Super skills** you practice things which are important in everyday life. What Super skill do you practice in the Project in Unit 8?

3 **In which unit do you see photos 1–8?**

1 ________

2 ________

3 ________

4 ________

5 ________

6 ________

7 ________

8 ________

4 **Work in pairs. Complete the challenge.**

Classroom CHALLENGE

1 In which unit do you plan an ideal school schedule?
2 In which unit do you learn to describe animals?
3 In which unit do you listen to a hockey player?
4 Where do you 'Think – Prepare – Practice – Perform' in every unit?
5 In which unit do you visit Comic Con?
6 What are the four steps in the final Writing activity?

How quickly can you find the answers?

7 In which unit do you study modal verbs of obligation?
8 In which unit do you talk about vacations?
9 In which unit do you give a presentation on a hero?
10 Where do you learn Super skills?
11 In which Project do you make a mini-book?
12 In which unit do you study food vocabulary?

1 School life

WDYT? (What do you think?)

What is an ideal school?

Vocabulary: daily routines; school subjects

Grammar: simple present; object pronouns

Reading: an online article about online schools

Listening: a conversation with a Finnish student

Speaking: working together to check answers

Writing: a blog post

Project: design a schedule for your ideal school

Video skills p13

Real-world speaking p19

Project pp22–23

At my school in France, we have two hours for lunch. Some students **1** ______________ home, but others **2** ______________ lunch in the school cafeteria. There are no packed lunches!

In Brazil, some students **4** ______________ school at seven o'clock in the morning and **5** ______________ at 12 o'clock. My school is different. We study from 12 o'clock until five in the afternoon.

I'm from Ghana and in my family we **6** ______________ at four o'clock in the morning. I often help at home before I **7** ______________ to school. I walk 6 km to and from school because there isn't a bus.

Daily routines

1 When do students usually do the activities in the box? Complete the table.

~~do homework~~ finish school get up go home go to bed go to school have breakfast have dinner have lunch start school

Morning	Afternoon	Evening
		do homework

2 Complete the facts on the map with words from exercise 1.

3 Work in pairs. What things are similar and different in your school day?

Students at my school in Finland have less than four hours of class a day, and we only 3 ______________________ about 30 minutes of homework in the evening.

My typical day

1 On school days, I **wake up** at six fifteen, and get up five minutes later. I **take a shower** and **brush my hair**.

2 I have breakfast – noodles or oatmeal – at about six forty-five. I **brush my teeth** and then I go to school with my friends.

3 I **get dressed** in my school uniform and I **pack my bag** for school. I usually **make my bed** and **clean my room**, but sometimes I forget!

4 We start school at seven thirty and **take a break** at nine fifty. We all do physical exercises together.

5 We have lunch at twelve thirty and finish school at four o'clock. I go home and **get changed** into my regular clothes.

6 I have dinner with my family at about five thirty, and then I do homework for about three hours. I go to bed at ten o'clock and **go to sleep** – I'm usually really tired!

4 **Read about a Chinese student's typical day. Match paragraphs 1–6 with pictures A–F.**

A __

B __

C __

D __

E __

F __

5 **Match the times with the activities from a Chinese student's typical day.**

A 12:30 B 22:00 C 17:30 D 9:50

E 16:00 F 6:15 G 6:45 H 7:30

6 **Put the activities in the order you do them on a typical day.**

1 make my bed / wake up / get up
2 brush my hair / get dressed / take a shower
3 have breakfast / make my bed / brush my teeth
4 take a break / pack my bag / start school
5 go to sleep / go to bed / brush my teeth

Time and day

Use *at* with times – *at six thirty, at ten o'clock*
Use *in* with parts of the day – *in the morning, in the afternoon, in the evening* BUT *at night*
Use *on* with days – *on Monday(s), on Tuesday(s)*

7 **Complete the sentences with *at*, *in* or *on*.**

1 We finish school early ________ Fridays.
2 I sometimes take a shower ________ the evening.
3 I usually have breakfast ________ about seven o'clock.
4 I brush my teeth ________ the morning and ________ night.
5 My first class ________ Monday morning is math.

VIDEO SKILLS

8 **Watch the video. What daily activities do you see students do?**

9 **Work in pairs. Discuss the questions.**

1 Why did the vlogger make the video?
2 Who do you think this video is for?
3 How does the vlogger make the video interesting? Think about: how long you see each image, the music, her voice, etc.

An online article

1 **Match the words in the box with photos A–J. Then order them for a typical day.**

get dressed   get up   go home   go to school
go to sleep   have lunch   pack my bag
start school   take a break   wake up

A ____________________

B ____________________

C ____________________

D ____________________

E ____________________

F ____________________

G ____________________

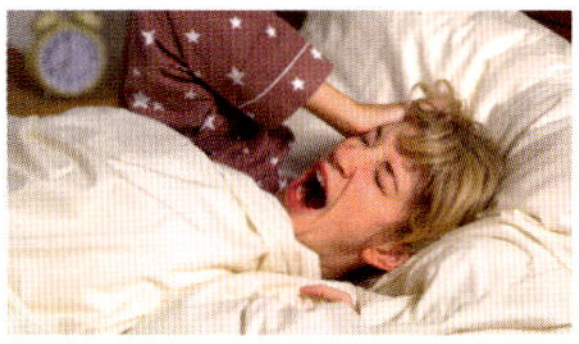

H ____________________

I ____________________

J ____________________

▶ Subskill: Predicting from the title and the pictures

Look at photos and the title of a text before you read to help you understand what it's about.

2 **Look at the photos on p15 and read the title of the article. Answer the questions.**

1 What day and time is it in the photos?
2 Why are the students at home?
3 What daily routine activities do you think the students do? What don't they do?

3 🔊 7 **Read and listen to the article. What daily routine activities do the students do?**

4 **Read the article again. Are the sentences true or false? Correct the false sentences.**

1 An online school has classes at fixed times.
2 Students see the whiteboard on their computer.
3 They can communicate with the teacher.
4 Students work on the computer all day.
5 They see their classmates outside school.
6 Online students study different subjects from students in other schools.

5 **Complete the sentences.**

1 Jack starts school at ____________________
2 Abi has her first class at ____________________
3 In the morning, they have ____________________
4 They have lunch, and then they ____________________
5 Jack learns about ____________________
6 They see friends in ____________________

6 **Word work** **Match the definitions to the words in bold in the text.**

1 numbers or letters that show how good schoolwork is ________
2 things you learn at school, e.g. math or English ________
3 a place where you can borrow or read books ________
4 start to use a computer ________
5 students in your class ________
6 visits with other students ________

7 **Complete with words from exercise 6.**

1 We sometimes go on ________ to museums or other places of interest.
2 There's a big ________ at my school with books.
3 Our teacher gives us ________ from one to ten for our homework.
4 The first thing we in do in computer classes is ________ .
5 I walk to school with one of my ________ .
6 We have science ________ every Friday.

CRITICAL THINKING — **SUPER SKILLS**

1 **Understand** Think about online and traditional schools. Find two things that are the same and two things that are different.

2 **Evaluate** Which of these things is an advantage of an online school? Which is a disadvantage?

3 **Create** Think of three advantages of a traditional school.

A DAY IN THE LIFE OF AN ONLINE STUDENT

Every year, more and more teens study at online high schools. They don't go to school like other students. They stay at home and connect to classes via the internet. So, what is a typical day for an online student?

The fact is, it depends. Students have classes, but they can study when they want. Jack wakes up at seven and reads for an hour before breakfast. He starts his classes at nine. Abi prefers to start school early, so she has free time for sports and other activities in the afternoon.

'I get up and **log on** for my first class at eight' she says. 'I read the notes on the whiteboard on my computer.' Abi doesn't see her teachers, but she can hear them. Later, she can ask questions online or by phone.

Both Jack and Abi have four classes in the morning. After lunch, they do homework and class projects. 'I don't sit at the computer all day,' says Jack. 'I make robots, or I go to the **library** and learn about the things I like.'

Of course, online students don't see their **classmates** every day. They sometimes go on **school trips** together, but they only meet friends in after-school clubs. They also need to be motivated, because they spend a lot of time studying alone.

In other ways, online schools are the same as ordinary schools. 'We study all the regular **subjects** like math and history,' says Abi. 'We take tests and we get **grades** for our work.'

Click here to find out what other students say about online learning.

CELEBRITY CORNER

Actor **Iain Armitage** doesn't go to school. He learns at home or in the TV studio with a 'studio teacher'. Which TV shows does he star in?

Simple present: affirmative and negative

1 Read the examples. Complete the table with the verbs in blue.

I **get up** at eight.
They **don't go** to school. They **stay** at home.
Jack **wakes up** at seven.
Abi **doesn't see** her teachers.
I **don't sit** at the computer all day.

Affirmative		
I/You	get up	at eight.
He/She/It	1	at seven.
We/They	2	at home.
Negative		
I/You	3	at the computer all day.
He/She/It	4	her teachers.
We/They	don't go	to school.

2 Circle the correct option.

1 We **don't/doesn't** go to school on Saturdays.
2 Many students **start/starts** school before nine o'clock.
3 My younger brother **don't study/doesn't study** on weekends.
4 Our school **open/opens** at eight thirty.
5 I **don't/doesn't** do homework in the morning.
6 Our school year **start/starts** in September.

3 Read the Spelling rules on p21. Write the third person singular of the verbs in the box.

finish get up go have
make play study watch

4 Complete the sentences with the simple present form of the verbs in parentheses.

1 I (...) **(wake up)** at seven o'clock but I (...) **(not get up)** until seven fifteen.
2 My brother (...) **(not make)** his bed on school days. My dad (...) **(make)** it.
3 I (...) **(have)** cereal for breakfast but my mom (...) **(have)** toast.
4 My sister (...) **(go)** to school before me.
5 Our teacher (...) **(give)** us homework, but we (...) **(not get)** much on weekends.
6 My brother (...) **(study)** for hours every day.

5 Change the underlined words to make the sentences true for you.

1 I go to <u>an online school</u>.
I don't go to an online school. I go to a ...
2 My school day starts at <u>11 o'clock</u>.
3 We take a break at <u>nine thirty</u>.
4 I study English on <u>Sundays</u>.
5 My school day finishes at <u>six o'clock</u>.
6 <u>My parents</u> do my homework.

6 8 Complete the text with the correct form of the verbs. Then listen and check.

Can you imagine going to a school like HOGWARTS?

In many ways, Hogwarts, in the Harry Potter books, is a regular boarding school. A typical day **1** ________ **(start)** with breakfast in the Great Hall. Then a bell **2** ________ **(ring)** and the students go to class. They **3** ________ **(have)** two classes before lunch, and two more classes in the afternoon. They even **4** ________ **(do)** homework, take exams, and they get grades for their work.

But students **5** ________ **(not study)** regular subjects, they learn about magic. And Harry **6** ________ **(not play)** soccer, he plays quidditch.

You probably think that schools like Hogwarts **7** ________ **(not exist)**, but there is a real-life wizardry school in California. It **8** ________ **(teach)** students all about magic!

7 Answer the question to solve the Brain teaser.

BRAIN TEASER

	School start time			Likes		
	8:00	8:45	9:15	chess	music	dance
Tom						
Ana						
Sara						

1 Tom starts school before Ana.
2 Sara likes dance. She is the first to start school.
3 Ana doesn't like chess.

What do you know about Tom, Ana and Sara?
(Clue: each answer is true for only one student.)

School subjects

1 **Look at the extract from a school schedule and find ...**

1 two sciences ______________________________

2 one creative subject ______________________

3 one foreign language _____________________

Class B	MONDAY	TUESDAY	WEDNESDAY
9:30–10:10	math	English literature	chemistry
10:10–10:50	history	French	math
10:50–11:10		BREAK	
11:10–11:50	biology	technology	technology
11:50–12:30	P.E.	math	P.E.
12:30–1:10		LUNCH BREAK	
1:10–2:00	basketball practice		
2:00–2:40	design	music	geography
2:40–3:20	English language	music	civics
Homework	math English biology	French math	chemistry math geography

2 **Add the following subjects to groups 1–3 in exercise 1.**

art drama German physics

3 🔊9 **Listen to extracts 1–6 and match each one to a subject from the schedule.**

4 **Work in pairs. Tell your partner which is your favorite day on the schedule and why.**

Which is your favorite day?

Tuesday, because I like French and they have music twice.

A conversation

Hi! I'm Ansa. I'm from Hamina in Finland but this month I'm in York, England, visiting family and going to a British school.

Subskill: Identifying the type of listening

To identify the type of listening, think about: people (how many?), places (where are they?) and language (is it formal or informal?).

5 🔊10 **Listen and circle the correct description.**

a An interview with Ansa on local radio

b Ansa talking to a teacher

c A dialogue between Ansa and a classmate

6 **Listen again. Which sentences are true?**

1 Ansa thinks school in Britain is similar to her school.

2 Ansa starts school at half past eight.

3 Ansa has school after lunch.

4 Ansa doesn't have any exams.

5 In a project, all the students work on the same thing.

6 Finnish students study subjects in separate lessons.

7 **Correct the false sentences in exercise 6.**

8 **Work in pairs. Would you like to go to Ansa's school? Why/Why not?**

I'd like to go to Ansa's school because I'd like to do projects.

Really? I prefer to study separate subjects.

FUN FACTS

In Finland, students start school when they're seven years old.

Pronunciation: Silent letters p128

Simple present: *Yes/No* questions

1 Read the examples. Complete the table.

Do you **have** history classes in school? Yes, we **do**.
Does your school **start** later? No, it **doesn't**.
Do you **go** back in the afternoon? No, I **don't**.

***Yes/No* questions and short answers**		
Do	I / 1 ________ /we/they	**think** it's different?
Yes, No,		2 ________ . **don't**.
3 ________	he/she/it	**start** at eight o'clock?
4 ________ , No,		**does**. 5 ________ .

2 Match the questions with the short answers in the box.

Yes, she does. Yes, I do. Yes, we do.
No, it doesn't. No, they don't.

1 Does your school have a swimming pool?
2 Do you and your classmates study French?
3 Do the students wear a uniform?
4 Does your teacher use a computer?
5 Do you like your school?

3 Write questions. Use *Do* or *Does*.

1 you / start school / eight o'clock ?
Do you start school at eight o'clock?
2 your class / study / German ?
3 you / have classes / Saturdays ?
4 your school / finish / 3:30 ?
5 your teachers / give / homework ?

4 Work in pairs. Take turns to ask the questions and answer with short answers.

Object pronouns

5 Complete the table with the object pronouns in the box.

We present **them**.
I can't imagine studying **it**.

her him it me us you

Subject	I	you	he	she	it	we	they
Object	1	2	3	4	5	6	*them*

6 Replace the words in bold with an object pronoun.

1 P.E. is my favorite class – I love **P.E.**!
2 Our art teacher, Mr. Flynn, is great – we like **Mr. Flynn** a lot.
3 I think science subjects are really difficult. I don't like **science subjects**.
4 I go to school with Sara and I come home with **Sara** too.
5 Our math teacher always gives **our class** lots of homework.

7 Circle the correct option.

GRAMMAR ROUND-UP

1 2 3 4 5 6 7 8

Teach yourself!

If you 1 **want/wants** to learn something new, why not use your phone? You 2 **can download/can to download** lots of great learning apps and use 3 **they/them** to learn all kinds of things, from languages to computer coding.

Are you into video? *Magisto* and *Openshot*™ are great apps to learn video editing. If 4 **you no know/you don't know** how to do your design homework, then *Instructables*® is the app for you. *WikiHow* is a great option too! And if you 5 **want/do want** help with art, go for *MyPaint* or *Krita*. They 6 **do have/have** some fantastic ideas to help you.

7 **Do they cost/Cost they** a lot of money? 8 **No, they don't cost./No, they don't.** Most of the apps are free.

Research

Find one of the apps in the article online. Would it be useful for you?

Working together to check answers

1 **Look at four things students do in class. In which activities do you work together?**

- **a** playing a game
- **b** taking an exam
- **c** checking answers to an exercise
- **d** asking what the homework is

2 **Watch the video. What is the activity? Choose from a–d in exercise 1.**

3 **Watch again. Which Key phrases do you hear?**

4 **Complete the dialogue with the Key phrases. Watch again and check.**

Carmel: What **1** _________ number 1? I've got 'Australia'.

Lukas: Yes, me too. OK – what about number 2? I've got 'Sydney'.

Carmel: Are you **2** _________ ? I've got 'Canberra'. Let's leave that one.

Lukas: OK, and number 3? The number of states ...

Carmel: I don't **3** _________ .

Lukas: I think it's 'six'.

Carmel: OK, six. Now, number 4. I **4** _________ it's '34 million'.

Lukas: Are you sure? I've got '24 million'.

Carmel: Oops, yes, you're **5** _________ . I can't read my writing!

Lukas: Right. Number 5 – the national sport. Do **6** _________ think it's 'rugby'?

Carmel: Let's see ... 'rugby'! High five!

5 **Create your own dialogue. Follow the steps in the Skills boost.**

SKILLS BOOST

THINK
Work individually. You have five minutes to complete the Geography quiz below.

PREPARE
In pairs, use your answers to the quiz to prepare a dialogue of students checking together. Remember to use the Key phrases for working together.

PRACTICE
Practice your dialogue.

PERFORM
Act out your dialogue for the class.

Geography quiz

1. Which city is not in Canada: Montreal, Seattle or Toronto?
2. Is the Antarctic in the north or the south?
3. What's the next planet: Mercury, Venus, Earth, ... ?
4. Which is the capital of Turkey: Ankara or Istanbul?
5. On which continent is Mount Kilimanjaro?

6 **Peer review** **Listen to your classmates and answer the questions.**

1. Which Key phrases do they use?
2. Do you agree with their answers to the quiz?

Key phrases

Asking about a question: What about number ... ?
What have you got for number ... ?
Do you think it's ... ?

Giving your answer: I've got ...
I think it's ...

Agreeing on the same answer: Yes, me too.
You're right.

Disagreeing (you have a different answer):
Really? I've got ...
Are you sure?

Saying you don't know the answer: I don't know.

UK → US

I**'ve got** 'Australia'. (UK) → I **have** 'Australia'. (US)

Tell us about your school

All About My School is an international project where teachers and students from different countries post descriptions about school life where they live and answer questions from students in other countries.

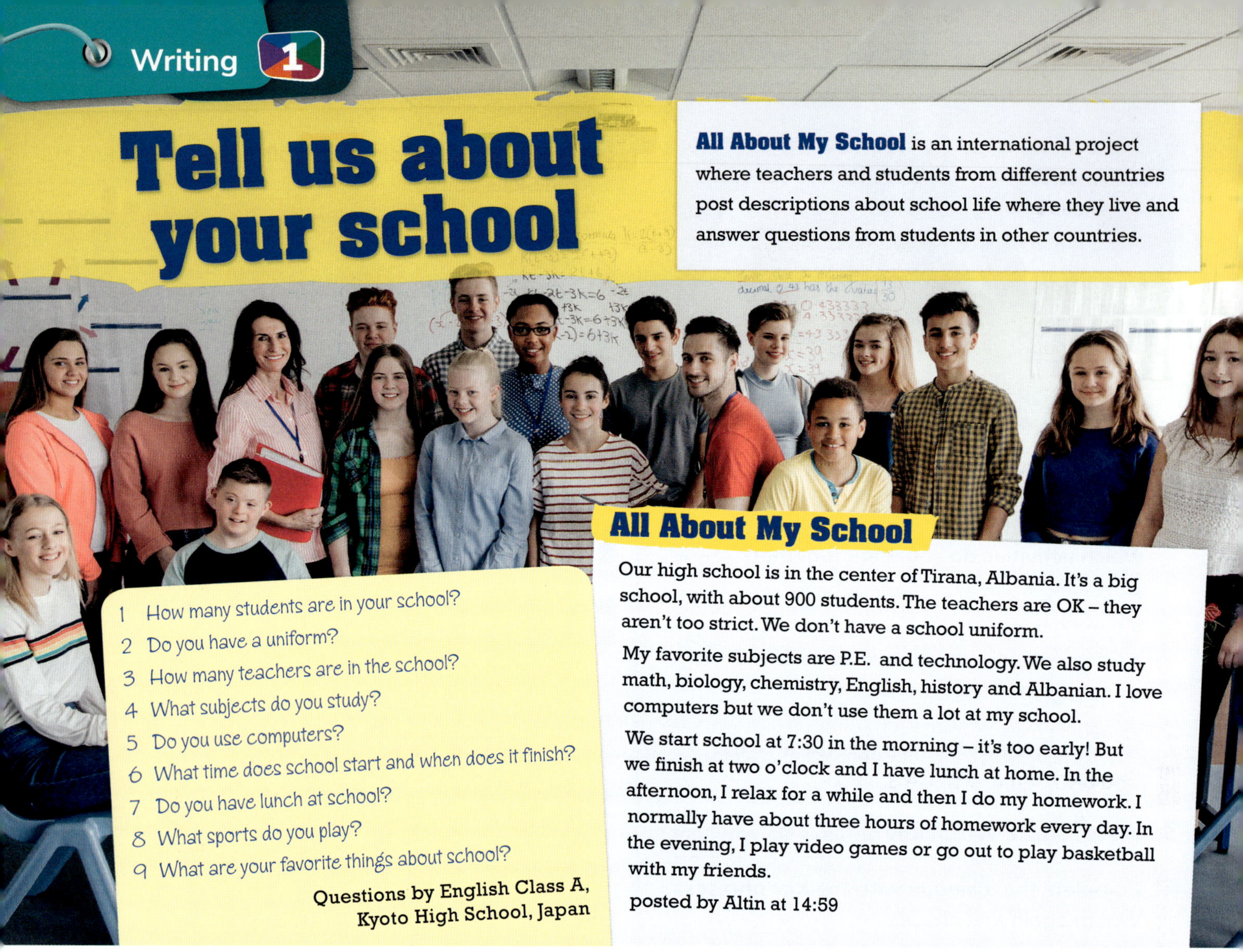

1 How many students are in your school?
2 Do you have a uniform?
3 How many teachers are in the school?
4 What subjects do you study?
5 Do you use computers?
6 What time does school start and when does it finish?
7 Do you have lunch at school?
8 What sports do you play?
9 What are your favorite things about school?

Questions by English Class A,
Kyoto High School, Japan

All About My School

Our high school is in the center of Tirana, Albania. It's a big school, with about 900 students. The teachers are OK – they aren't too strict. We don't have a school uniform.

My favorite subjects are P.E. and technology. We also study math, biology, chemistry, English, history and Albanian. I love computers but we don't use them a lot at my school.

We start school at 7:30 in the morning – it's too early! But we finish at two o'clock and I have lunch at home. In the afternoon, I relax for a while and then I do my homework. I normally have about three hours of homework every day. In the evening, I play video games or go out to play basketball with my friends.

posted by Altin at 14:59

A blog post

1 **Read the questions and answers in the blog. Does the writer answer all the questions?**

2 **Read the blog post again and find the answers to questions 1–9 in Altin's answer.**

3 **Match a–c with each paragraph in the blog.**

a Subjects
b School day and free time
c General description of the school, the students and teachers

Subskill: Capital letters

In English, some words have a capital letter. Remember that it isn't just the first word at the start of a sentence, e.g. *I have a French class on Monday.*

4 **Read the school subjects. Find two rules for using capital letters.**

art English French geography technology math P.E.

5 **Read the list. When do we use a capital letter in English?**

a for I, e.g. *Can I use your pen?* ✓
b at the start of a sentence
c for all nouns
d for days of the week
e for greetings
f for months of the year
g for names and surnames
h for people's titles
i for cities, countries and nationalities

6 **Work in pairs. Read Altin's description and explain the reason for each capital letter.**

7 **Correct the text, adding capital letters where necessary.**

Hi
~~hi~~! i'm pearl. i live in edinburgh, in scotland. the school year here starts in august and finishes in june. we have classes five days a week, from monday to friday. my favorite subjects are p.e. and german. all our teachers are very nice but my favorite is our biology teacher, mr. liddle.

8 Write an entry about your school life for the *All About My School* blog. Follow the steps in the Skills boost.

SKILLS BOOST

THINK

Write your answers to the questions in *All About My School.*

1 ______
2 ______
3 ______
4 ______
5 ______
6 ______
7 ______
8 ______
9 ______

PREPARE

Organize the information from your answers into three paragraphs. Use the paragraph headings and order from exercise 3.

Paragraph 1: ______

Paragraph 2: ______

Paragraph 3: ______

WRITE

Write your blog post. Use Altin's post to help you.

CHECK

Answer the questions.

1 Is the blog post interesting to read? ☐
2 Do you use paragraphs? ☐
3 Do you use the simple present correctly? ☐
4 Do you use capital letters correctly? ☐

9 Peer review **Exchange your blog post with another student. Does the writer give clear information about school life in your country?**

Quick review

Grammar

Simple present

Affirmative

With *he/she/it* the verb ends in *-s*, *-es* or *-ies*.

*I **get up** at seven o'clock.* *She **goes** to sleep at 10:30.*

Negative

I/you/we/they: subject + *don't* + verb
he/she/it: subject + *doesn't* + verb

*We **don't have** a school uniform.* *He **doesn't study** French.*

Yes/No questions and short answers

Do + *I/you/we/they* + verb?	Yes, I/you/we/they do.
	No, I/you/we/they don't.
Does + *he/she/it* + verb?	Yes, he/she/it does.
	No, he/she/it doesn't.
***Do** they **study** music?*	*Yes, they **do**.*
***Does** the school **have** a gym?*	*No, it **doesn't**.*

Spelling rules for *he/she/it*

For most verbs, add *-s*:
read → he reads *wake up → she wakes up*
For verbs that end in *-s*, *-sh*, *-ss*, *-ch*, *-x* or *-o*, add *-es*:
go → it goes *teach → she teaches* *mix → he mixes*
For verbs that end in consonant + *y*, omit the *y* and add *-ies*:
study → he studies
Some verbs are irregular: *have → she **has***

Subject and object pronouns

Subject pronouns: I, you, he, she, it, we, they
Object pronouns: me, you, him, her, it, us, them

***I** start my homework at six o'clock and finish **it** at seven.*
*Can **you** help **us**?*

Vocabulary

11 Daily routines

brush my hair, brush my teeth, clean my room, do homework, finish school, get changed, get dressed, get up, go home, go to bed, go to school, go to sleep, have breakfast, have dinner, have lunch, make my bed, pack my bag, start school, take a break, take a shower, wake up

12 School subjects

art, biology, chemistry, civics, design, drama, English language, English literature, French, geography, German, history, math, music, P.E., physics, technology

1 Project

WDYT?
(What do you think?)

What is an ideal school?

TASK: Design a schedule for your ideal school.

Learning outcomes

1 I can talk about the importance of different school subjects.

2 I can make logical decisions.

3 I can use appropriate language from the unit.

Graphic organizer → Project planner p130

1 Watch a video of students talking about their ideal timetable, or schedule. What's the first lesson, or class, of the week?

STEP 1: THINK

2 Look at the photos and the schedule in the Model project. What school subjects can you see in the photos?

3 What do you learn in these subjects? Match 1–4 with a–d.

1 money management	a how to speak to a group of people
2 cyber-security	b how to be safe online
3 public speaking	c how to create new things
4 inventing	d how to use money

4 Are the subjects useful? Why/Why not?

STEP 2: PLAN

5 Work in pairs. Read the tips in the Super skills box and practice saying the Key phrases with a partner.

CRITICAL THINKING — SUPER SKILLS

Making logical decisions

Tips

Don't make a quick decision.

List the advantages and disadvantages.

Think about the advantages and disadvantages before you decide.

Key phrases

Wait a moment. *Yes, but don't forget ...*

Slow down. *I'd like to learn ...*

What about ... ? *Me too.*

I think/don't think that's a good thing.

Really? I'd prefer ...

6 Work in pairs. Make notes about your ideal school schedule. Use the tips and Key phrases in the Super skills box.

- the time of the school day – when it starts and finishes
- the number of minutes for each class
- the school subjects that you want to study

STEP 3: CREATE

7 In your notebook, prepare a schedule for a week of classes.

8 Write sentences about your school schedule. Explain your decisions.

Our school day starts at ... and finishes at ... because ...

Our first class is ...

We think it's ...

Students learn music because we think ...

Grammar and Vocabulary Quick review p21

Model project

A

B

	MONDAY	TUESDAY	WEDNESDAY
9:00–9:50	yoga	app design	martial arts
9:50–10:40	Chinese	science	math
10:40–11:00		BREAK	
11:00–11:50	chemistry	inventing	money management
11:50–12:40	history	English	cyber-security
12:40–13:30	movie-making	cooking	public speaking
13:30		LUNCH/GO HOME	

C

D

STEP 4: PRESENT

9 Read the How to ... tips on p130. Then work with another pair. Tell them about your school schedule.

10 Peer review Choose the schedule you think is most interesting and useful for all students.

1 FINAL REFLECTION

1 The task

How well can you describe your ideal school schedule?

Can you explain your decisions? Give examples.

2 Super skill

Are your decisions logical? Say why.

3 Language

Do you use language from the unit? Give examples.

2 Me time

WDYT?
(What do you think?)

How important are hobbies for teenagers?

Vocabulary: free-time activities; collocations with *do*, *go* and *play*

Grammar: adverbs of frequency; likes and dislikes; simple present: *Wh-* questions

Reading: a blog about a champion skateboarder

Listening: a radio interview with a hockey player

Speaking: asking for information

Writing: informal messages

Project: do a survey about how students spend their free time

Video skills p25

Real-world speaking p31

Project pp34–35

Free-time activities

1 Work in pairs. Read the statistics. Does any of the information surprise you?

> I'm surprised American teenagers sleep for nearly 11 hours.

> Really? I'm not that surprised. I think ...

2 Complete the table with the free-time activities in red.

Media and communication	Sports	Art and music	Other

3 Which free-time activities in the box do you see in photos 1–6? Add them all to the table in exercise 2.

collect things | draw | go to a dance class | go to the gym | help at home | make videos | play chess | play in a band | play on a team | practice the piano | use social media

1 ____________ 2 ____________ 3 ____________

4 ____________ 5 ____________ 6 ____________

4 Complete the description with words and phrases from exercise 3. Change the form of the verb if necessary.

My brother Archie and I are twins but we're very different. I'm really into sports. I love soccer and I **1** ____________ called the Midland Juniors. I have to bet quick and strong for soccer, so I also **2** ____________ once a week.

Archie is very musical. He plays the guitar and he sometimes **3** ____________ for three hours a day. On weekends, he **4** ____________ with two friends.

We both **5** ____________ on our phones to chat with our friends and sometimes we **6** ____________ to put on YouTube™.

But it isn't all fun! On weekends, we also do homework and **7** ____________ .

5 How many hours do you spend on free-time activities on the weekend?

social media – 2 hours *soccer – 1 hour*

6 Work in pairs. Talk about your free-time activities using your notes in exercise 5.

VIDEO SKILLS

7 Watch the video. What activities does the vlogger do on the weekend?

8 Work in pairs. Discuss the questions.

1 Which elements of the video help you to understand it? Think about images, text and the presenter.
2 Why are vloggers popular?
3 Would you like to be a vlogger? Why/Why not?

A blog

1 13 **Listen to people doing seven free-time activities. Which activities do you hear?**

2 Look at the photos on p27. Which of the things in the box can you see?

ball girl graffiti hat people watching skateboard swimming pool table

3 Look at the text, but don't read it. What type of text is it? Explain your answer.

a a newspaper article
b part of a novel
c a blog post

4 14 **Read and listen to the text and circle the best summary.**

a Brighton has lots of hobbies.
b Brighton is a normal girl with a special talent.
c Brighton has a busy life.

Subskill: Reading for specific information

To find specific information in a text, first identify key words in the exercise that will help you.

5 Read the text again and complete the sentences.

1 Brighton is ________ years old.
2 She studies in ________ grade.
3 One of her favorite musicians is ________ .
4 She likes watching videos on ________ .
5 She's extremely good at ________ .
6 She practices before and ________ school every day.
7 She feels ________ before competitions.

6 Match 1–5 to a–e to make sentences.

1 At home, Brighton does	a sport at the Olympics®.
2 Brighton is only 13, but	b some things about being famous.
3 Skateboarding is a new	c she's a champion in adult competitions.
4 Brighton doesn't like	d she's a normal teenager too.
5 Brighton is famous but	e the same things as other teenagers.

7 Word work Match the definitions to the words in bold in the text.

1 a very famous actor, singer or athlete ________
2 practices (a sport) seriously ________
3 fantastic, surprising ________
4 (in sports) for young people, not adults ________
5 a person who wins a competition ________
6 excited and worried at the same time ________

8 Work in pairs. Ask and answer the questions.

Do you know anyone who ... ?

- trains regularly with a sports team
- gets nervous before doing something
- can take amazing photos
- is a champion swimmer

CRITICAL THINKING — SUPER SKILLS

1 **Understand** Read the text. Find one way that Brighton's life is like a typical teenager's and one way in which it is different.

2 **Evaluate** If you become very good at a hobby, lots of things can change. Add some more advantages and disadvantages.

Advantages

You can train and improve your technique.

Disadvantages

It's expensive.

3 **Create** Imagine you can meet Brighton. Write three questions to ask her.

Work in groups of four.

Students A, B and C: Ask your questions.

Student D: You are Brighton. Use your imagination and answer the questions!

Research

What other sports are in the X-Games? Find out about one of them and present it to the class.

CELEBRITY CORNER

A young tennis player with a special talent is **Cori 'Coco' Gauff**. She trains hard and inspires teenagers. Find out what she does in her free time.

At the top of her game

October 6th

THIS WEEK'S TALENTED TEEN IS BRIGHTON ZEUNER.

Brighton is 13. Like any other 8th grade student in the United States, in the evenings she usually does homework or listens to music in her bedroom. She likes Beyoncé. She hardly ever has free time but she loves watching videos on YouTube.

But Brighton, from Encinitas, California, is also an X-Games **champion** skateboarder. And not in a **junior** competition. No – Brighton is the world champion and competes against women twice her age. **Amazing**, right?

But the future looks even more exciting for Brighton. The big news is that skateboarding is now an Olympic sport! To prepare for the next X-Games and the Olympics, Brighton **trains** every morning before school, and in the afternoon she always practices in her local skate park.

Is it difficult to be famous when you're so young? Brighton says she is sometimes **nervous** when she gives interviews or before competitions, but it's all part of the sport she loves. And the great thing about Brighton is that she's a skateboarding **superstar**, but she's also a normal person like you or me.

Like Reply

October 6th | 7:45 pm

That's so cool! What an amazing example.

Suzy Skater

October 6th | 8:10 pm

Let's hope Brighton gets the gold at the Olympics!

MarioBlogs

October 6th | 10:13 pm

It's great that Brighton can still have a normal life.

Princess Carrie

Leave a comment

Enter your comment here:

Adverbs of frequency

1 Read the examples. Complete the table with the adverbs of frequency.

In the evenings she **usually** does homework or listens to music.

She **always** practices in her local skate park.

She is **sometimes** nervous when she gives interviews.

She **hardly ever** has free time.

More frequent ←→ Less frequent					
1	2	*often*	3	4	*never*

2 Read the sentences in exercise 1 again. Circle the correct option to complete the rules.

1 With the verb *be*, the adverb comes **before/ after** the verb.

2 With other verbs, the adverb comes **before/ after** the verb.

3 Rewrite the sentences with the adverbs of frequency in the correct position.

1 I am home late on Mondays. **(always)**

I am always home late on Mondays.

2 Frankie practices the piano for hours. **(often)**

3 Ahmed does his homework before playing video games. **(usually)**

4 They are tired after their dance class. **(sometimes)**

5 My sister takes lots of photos when we go on vacation. **(always)**

6 Lily helps her parents at home. **(hardly ever)**

7 My best friend is hungry after baseball practice. **(always)**

Likes and dislikes

4 Complete the table with the verbs in the box.

don't like don't mind hate ~~like~~ love

1	*like*	2	3	4

5 Read the examples. Complete the table with the words in the box.

She **likes** Beyoncé.

I **love** watching videos.

He **doesn't mind** practicing the piano.

doesn't mind love she verb *-ing* we

Subject	Verb	Noun, 3 ________
I/you/ 1 ________ / they	2 ________ /**like**/ **don't mind**/**don't like**/**hate**	tennis.
he/ 4 ________ / it	**loves**/**likes**/ 5 ________ / **doesn't like**/**hates**	sleeping.

6 Read the information and write sentences.

1 They  play / chess.

2 She  draw / manga comics.

3 I  Barcelona.

4 We  help / our parents.

5 He  play / video games.

7 Complete the text with the correct form of the words in parentheses.

American teenager Carissa Yip is an international chess champion – a grandmaster. She **1** ________ **(play / often)** in adult competitions and the adults **2** ________ **(be / sometimes)** angry when she wins. She **3** ________ **(lose / hardly ever)**. Carissa **4** ________ **(love / play)** chess but she also likes other things: she **5** ________ **(like / sushi)** and she **6** ________ **(love / play)** with her grandmother's cat when she visits China. Carissa also **7** ________ **(like / make)** videos and she **8** ________ **(post / often)** comments and videos on websites for chess fans.

8 Answer the question to solve the Brain teaser.

BRAIN TEASER

Jimmy and Jenny have lots of hobbies. They like swimming and they both like collecting things. They don't like sports or drawing. Jimmy loves sleeping and Jenny likes chess.

Do they like taking photos?
(Clue: think about the letters in the words!)

Reinforcement and Challenge Grammar bootcamp pp118–119

Collocations with *do*, *go* and *play*

1 **Read the ad. Is the sports center a good place for these people?**

1 I enjoy team sports.

2 I only like winter sports.

3 I want to do martial arts.

4 I like playing ball games.

5 I prefer water sports.

6 I love dancing.

2 **What sports can each person from exercise 1 play or do at the sports center?**

3 **Read the ad again. Complete the rules with *do*, *go* and *play*.**

1 We use _________ with ball sports.
2 We use _________ with verb *-ing*.
3 We use _________ with other activities.

4 **Complete the table with the activities from the ad. Then add the sports in the box.**

badminton biking gymnastics horseback riding ping-pong skateboarding skiing surfing track and field yoga

Do	Go	Play
karate		

5 **Work in pairs. Ask and answer questions about the activities in exercise 4.**

Do you play basketball?

Yes, I do. What about you?

A radio interview

Subskill: Listening for the general idea

When you listen for general understanding, wait until you finish listening before you answer.

6 15 **Listen to an interview with a hockey player. What does the player talk about?**

a how sports help you to keep fit
b the rules of field hockey
c the advantages of team sports

7 **Listen again. Why does Ben think hockey is a good sport? Which ideas does he mention?**

1 you learn to work on a team
2 you learn from mistakes
3 players help each other
4 it teaches you to work in groups
5 you learn to work hard
6 you learn to be organized

8 **Listen again and answer the questions.**

1 How old are the players on the hockey team?
2 How many players are on Ben's team?
3 When do they practice?
4 What other sport does he do?

9 **Work in pairs. Answer the questions.**

1 What are the advantages of individual sports?
2 Which do you prefer, team sports or individual sports? Why?

Simple present: *Wh-* questions

1 Copy the tables and add questions a–c.

a Why do you like field hockey?
b When have you got your next match?
c Who is the team captain?

be questions

Question word	am/ is/are	subject	
Why	**is**	hockey	important to you?
How old	**are**	the players?	

***have got* questions**

Question word	have/ has	subject	got	
How many people	**have**	you	**got**	on your team?
Why	**has**	the team	**got**	16 players?

Questions with other simple present verbs

Question word	do/does	subject	verb	
How	**does**	hockey	**help**	you?
When	**do**	you	**play**?	

2 Order the words to make questions.

1 you / have / P.E. / When / got ?
2 favorite / are / What / your / sports ?
3 keep fit / How / you / do ?
4 does / play / Where / your local football team ?
5 is / Who / your favorite athlete ?

3 Work in pairs. Ask and answer the questions in exercise 2.

4 Complete the questions with the correct words.

1 How ________ you say 40–40 in tennis?
a equals **b** deuce **c** forty-forty

2 What ________ surfing, skateboarding and karate got in common?
a They're adventure sports. **b** They come from Australia.
c They're Olympic sports.

3 What ________ the name of the New Zealand rugby team?
a All Whites **b** All Blacks **c** All Reds

4 When ________ the NBA basketball season usually begin?
a September **b** October **c** November

5 How many rings ________ on the Olympic flag?
a five **b** six **c** seven

5 16 **Circle the correct answers in the quiz. Listen and check.**

6 Write questions with *is, are, do, does* and *have got*.

1 What / you / do in your free time ?
2 When / you / do it ?
3 How many video games / you ?
4 What / your favorite game ?
5 Why / you / like it ?

7 Work in pairs. Ask and answer the questions in exercise 6.

8 Circle the correct option.

GRAMMAR ROUND-UP

1 2 3 4 5 6 7 8

What game **1 do/does** you play with a field hockey ball and a bicycle? The answer is simple: bike polo.

Bike polo is over 100 years old. It **2 come/comes** from Ireland, but now it's popular all over the world.

People **3 usually play/play usually** polo on horses, but in this sport all you need is a bike. It **4 doesn't cost/don't cost** a lot of money, and each team **5 has/have** only got three players.

Brendan Fox, aged 15, loves **6 play/playing** bike polo. You can see **7 he/him** on his bike every day after school. Why **8 does he like/he likes** it? 'Well, it **9 is sometimes/sometimes is** a bit dangerous,' he says, 'but it's really fun.'

Pronunciation: *do you* /djʊ/ p128

Reinforcement and Challenge Grammar bootcamp p119

Asking for information

1 **Look at the brochure. Which course would you like to do?**

2 **Watch the video. Which course does Maria choose?**

3 **Complete the dialogue with the Key phrases. Watch again and check.**

Maria
Excuse me. Hi. I'd like to **1** ____________ your courses, please.

Receptionist
Oh, hello. Yes, of course.

Maria
2 ____________ a photography course?

Receptionist
Just one moment. Yes, we do. It's on Mondays, from 6 to 7:30.

Maria
That isn't good for me. I always play basketball on Mondays.

Receptionist
We have a painting class on Wednesdays.

Maria
I don't like painting. Thanks anyway.

Receptionist
What about movie-making? That's on Thursdays, from 4:30 to 5:30.

Maria
3 ____________ is it?

Receptionist
Let's see. It's $75 for ten classes, but the first class is free.

Maria
Great! Can I **4** ____________ ?

Receptionist
Of course, just one moment ...

Let's cook! Street food
5:00–6:00 pm
Photography
6:00–7:30 pm

TUESDAY
Yoga
4:30–5:30 pm
Easy robotics
5:30–7:00 pm

WEDNESDAY
Painting for beginners
4:00–5:30 pm

THURSDAY
Movie-making
4:30–5:30 pm
Chess
5:00–6:00 pm

FRIDAY
Drawing masterclass
3:30–4:30 pm
Coding and app building
7:00–9:00 pm

4 **Create your own dialogue. Follow the steps in the Skills boost.**

SKILLS BOOST

THINK
Choose an activity from the brochure, or think of another activity.

PREPARE
Prepare a dialogue. Use the information about days and times from the brochure, or use your own ideas.

PRACTICE
Practice your dialogue. Take turns to ask for and give information.

PERFORM
Act out your dialogue for the class.

5 **Peer review** **Listen to your classmates and answer the questions.**

1 What activity do they choose?
2 What questions do they use to ask for information?

Key phrases

I'd like to find out about your courses, please.
Can you tell me about your photography course?
What time does it start?
How much is it?
Do you have a ... course?
Can I sign up for it?
What day is it on?

US → UK

Do you have a photography course? (US)
→ Have you got a photography course? (UK)

Writing 2

A

Hi everyone!

My name's Akio and I'm from Japan. I'd love to have a pen pal. I like all kinds of sports. I do karate and I love watching baseball. Baseball is very popular in Japan. Do you like sports? Who is your favorite athlete? What sports are popular in your country? Hope to hear from you soon!

B

CALLING ALL STUDENTS!

We want to find out what people do in their free time for a class project. We need your help!

How do you spend your free time? What are your hobbies and why do you like them?

Please write us a short note and send it to Nick and Ava.

Cheers!

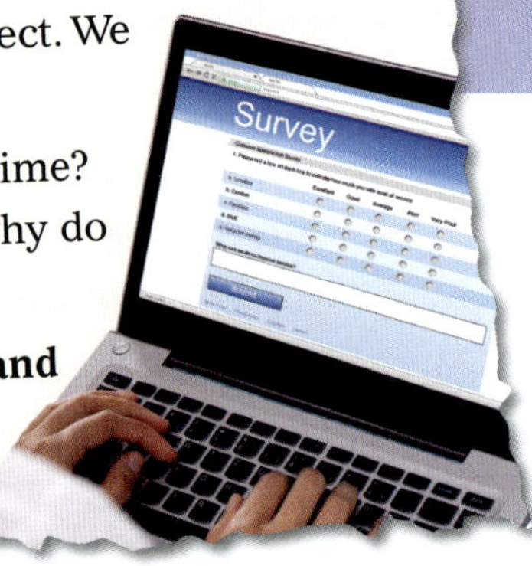

C

Hi Ed!

I'd like to find out about the Tech Club. I know you're a member. When does the club meet? Where do you have the club? What exactly do you do in it?

Let me know!

Ciara

Informal messages

1 **Read the messages and answer the questions.**

1 Who is each message to and from?

____

____

2 Why does each person write their message?

____

____

2 **Read the reply. Which message does it answer?**

Hi!

We meet on Thursdays after school at four. We usually finish at five, but we sometimes stay until five thirty. We meet in the computer lab, but most people bring their own laptops or tablets. Alex from Class 5A organizes the club and he's really great! He knows loads about coding. We do different things – it depends. We often work in groups. Some people create websites or blogs. Other people design apps. We all learn how to install software and solve problems with viruses.

Let me know if you want to go on Thursday. We can meet and go together.

See you soon!

3 **Read the reply in exercise 2 again and answer the questions from the original message.**

Subskill: *and*, *or* and *but*

We use and, or and but to connect ideas in a sentence.

4 **Find examples of *and*, *or* and *but* in the reply in exercise 2. Complete the rules.**

and   or   but

1 We use ________ to add a different idea.
2 We use ________ to add an alternative.
3 We use ________ to add a similar idea.

5 **Complete the sentences with *and*, *or* and *but*.**

1 On Saturday afternoons, I visit a friend. We go to her house ________ we meet in town.
2 I like playing sports, ________ I don't like watching them.
3 I like painting ________ I like drawing too.
4 I have a guitar lesson on Mondays ________ I go swimming on Thursdays.
5 Which do you prefer, soccer ________ basketball?
6 We sometimes go to the movies, ________ it's very expensive.

6 Write a message. Answer message A or B in exercise 1. Follow the steps in the Skills boost.

SKILLS BOOST

THINK

1 Choose message A or B.

2 What questions does the person ask?

____

____

3 What information do you need to give in your answer?

____

____

PREPARE

Make notes about your answers to the questions.

Question 1: ________________________

Question 2: ________________________

Question 3: ________________________

WRITE

Write your message.

Hi!/Hi Akio, ...

I usually ... in my free time.

CHECK

Read your message. Answer the questions.

1 Do you answer the three questions? ☐

2 Do you use adverbs of frequency (*usually, always, ...*)? ☐

3 Do you use verb *-ing* after *like, love, ...* ? ☐

4 Do you use *and, or* and *but* correctly? ☐

7 **Peer review** **Exchange your message with another student. Does the writer answer all the questions in the original message?**

Quick review

Grammar

Adverbs of frequency

always, usually, often, sometimes, hardly ever, never

be → adverb of frequency

*We're **never** late for class.*

*I'm **sometimes** nervous before exams.*

adverb of frequency → other verbs

*We **usually** watch TV in the evenings.*

*My friends and I **always** go to the skate park on the weekend.*

*My brother **hardly ever** plays sports.*

Likes and dislikes

love, like, don't mind, don't like, hate

... + verb *-ing*	... + noun
*I **love skateboarding**.*	*I **love sports**.*
*He **likes practicing** the piano.*	*He **likes music**.*
*I **don't mind drawing**.*	*I **don't mind art**.*
*We **don't like playing** chess.*	*We **don't like chess**.*
*They **hate watching** TV.*	*They **hate TV**.*

Question forms

Questions with *be*, *have got* and other verbs

Question word + *be* + subject

*Why **are you** late?* — ***I'm** late because ...*

*How old **is he**?* — ***He's** 14.*

Question word + *have/has* + subject + *got*

*What **have** you **got** in your bag?* — ***I've got** my laptop.*

*How many video games **has** he **got**?* — ***He's got** about 50.*

Question word + *do/does* + subject + base form

*How **do** you **go** to school?* — *I **go** to school by bus.*

*What time **does** the game **start**?* — *It **starts** at nine o'clock.*

Vocabulary

17 Free-time activities

collect things, draw, go to a dance class, go to the gym, help at home, listen to music, make videos, meet friends, play chess, play in a band, play on a team, play soccer, play video games, practice the piano, sleep, take photos, use social media, watch a TV series

18 Collocations with *do*, *go* and *play*

do: aerobics, gymnastics, hip hop, karate, martial arts, track and field, yoga

go: biking, horseback riding, roller-skating, skateboarding, skiing, surfing, swimming

play: badminton, basketball, field hockey, ping-pong, volleyball

2 Project

WDYT?
(What do you think?)

How important are hobbies for teenagers?

TASK: Do a survey about how students in the class spend their free time.

Learning outcomes

1 I can design a survey about free-time activities and summarise results.

2 I can organize a task with my classmates.

3 I can use appropriate language from the unit.

Graphic organizer → Project planner p130

1 Watch a video of students doing a survey. What's the topic of the survey?

STEP 1: THINK

2 Read the survey that the student uses in the Model project.

1 Find an example of a question which …
- a is a *Yes/No* question
- b gives options for answers
- c is open and has lots of possible answers

2 Which question word asks about … ?
- a people
- b things
- c time
- d reasons

STEP 2: PLAN

3 Work in groups. Read the tips in the Super skills box and practice saying the Key phrases with your group.

COLLABORATION — SUPER SKILLS

Planning and task management

Tips

Agree together how to organize things.

Make clear notes.

Use time effectively.

Key phrases

We can discuss first and then write.

What do you think?

Can you write down our ideas?

Let's write the questions in a different color.

OK, let's start.

We need to move to the next question.

4 Work in groups of three. Choose a topic for your survey. Use these ideas or your own. Use the tips and Key phrases in the Super skills box.
- creative hobbies (art, painting, drawing, photography)
- music
- social media
- socializing
- sports

5 Write at least six questions for your survey. Remember to include a variety of question types.

Do you like … ? *When do you usually … ?*

6 Each person chooses other classmates to ask. Ask the classmates your questions and note their answers.

STEP 3: CREATE

7 Read the summary of results in the Model project. Notice the expressions in bold.

Model project

FREE-TIME *activities survey*

1 Do you like playing computer games?
Yes ☐ No ☐

2 What games do you like playing?
______

3 How many hours a week do you spend playing games?
1–3 hours ☐ 4–10 hours ☐ more than 10 hours ☐

4 Who do you play games with?
a brother or sister ☐
friends ☐
other people online ☐

5 What is your favorite game?
______

6 Why do you like it?
______

FREE-TIME ACTIVITIES SURVEY *Class 1B*

Most students in the class like playing computer games. **Only four students** say they don't like playing games. **The most popular games are** adventure, action and sports games.

My classmates usually spend four to ten hours a week playing games. **Six people play** 1–3 hours a week, 14 people play 4–10 hours a week and nine people play more than ten hours a week.

They usually play with friends, **but they sometimes** play with people online. **Their favorite game is** the new Spider-Man game. It's fun and exciting.

8 In your group, compare the results of your survey.

9 Read the *How to ...* tips on p130. Then write a summary of your results.

STEP 4: PRESENT

10 Peer review Share your summaries and read other groups' results. How important are free-time activities for students in your class?

2 FINAL REFLECTION

1 The task
Do you ask different types of questions in your survey?
Is your summary clear and organized?

2 Super skill
Is your group effective at planning and organizing work together? Give examples.

3 Language
Do you use language from the unit? Give examples.

3 Dressing up

WDYT?
(What do you think?)

Why do people dress up?

Vocabulary: clothes and accessories; describing clothes

Grammar: present progressive; simple present and present progressive; time expressions

Reading: a live feed from Comic Con®

Listening: a live report about No Uniform Day

Speaking: shopping for clothes

Writing: photo descriptions

Project: make a mini-book about traditional clothes

Video skills p37

Real-world speaking p43

Project pp46–47

Clothes and accessories

1 Read the words in the box. Which ones can you see in the photos?

coat dress hat jacket jeans
pants shirt shoes skirt sneakers

2 Read the descriptions. Match descriptions 1–9 to photos A–I.

1 Ajay: a white **T-shirt** with a black and white shirt, jeans and a hat
2 Mickey: a red **hoodie** and black pants
3 Jenna: a blue and white top with **leggings** and sneakers
4 Erin: a white **top**, a pink **scarf**, pink pants and black **boots**
5 Collection 1: a blue and white top, blue **shorts**, sunglasses, a hat and pink **sandals**
6 Maya: red and black **tights** and black shoes
7 Collection 2: a brown **sweater**, boots, a pink hat, **sunglasses** and socks
8 Nicola: a black jacket, long pink skirt and a hat
9 Louis: a gray hoodie, blue jeans and yellow sneakers

3 Complete the table with the words in bold in exercise 2.

Head and neck	
Upper body	
Legs	
Feet	

Plurals

In English, *jeans*, *pants*, *shorts*, *tights* and *leggings* are plural.

I like these jeans. They're great!

4 19 **Listen to people talking about the photos. Which one are they describing?**

5 **Complete the sentences with the words in the box.**

boots coat hoodie leggings sandals shorts sneakers T-shirt

"I love shoes. In the summer I wear **1** ________ and when it's cold I wear **2** ________ . And of course, when I play sports I wear **3** ________ ."

"It's very cold today! That jacket's no good – wear your winter **4** ________ ."

"When I go running in the summer I usually wear a **5** ________ and **6** ________ , but if it's cold I wear **7** ________ and put on a **8** ________ as well."

6 **Work in pairs. Do you like any of the outfits in the photos?**

I like this one, because I like wearing sneakers and it's good for playing sports.

I don't like this one, because I'm not into wearing hoodies.

VIDEO SKILLS

7 **Watch the video and answer the questions.**

1 How are the clothes you see unusual?
2 Would you like to wear them? Why/Why not?

8 **Work in pairs. Discuss the questions.**

1 Why is the beginning in black and white?
2 What is the main reason for this video?
   a to be funny   b to sell something
   c to give information
3 What is the message of the video?
   a Fashion is about color.
   b There are different opinions about what fashion is.
   c Fashion is about art.

A live feed

1 **Work in pairs. Look at the photos on p39 and describe someone's clothes. Can your partner guess who it is?**

This person is wearing a hat and a sweater.

It's this man here.

You're right!

2 **Look at the photos again and answer the questions.**

1 What type of event can you see?
2 What happens there?
3 What type of people go there?

▶ Subskill: Identifying the text type

Identify the type of text before you read. This can help you predict and understand the content.

3 **Look at the text and answer the questions.**

1 What type of text is it?
2 Do you normally read this type of text ... ?
  a in a book
  b on a computer
  c on your phone
3 What is unusual about the order of the text?

4 20 **Read and listen to the text and match each message with a photo.**

5 **Are the sentences true or false? Find information in the text to support your answer.**

1 Comic Con isn't very busy at the start of the day.
2 The fans walk in slowly.
3 Some people are wearing unusual clothes.
4 In one part of the festival you can watch people draw.
5 Fans can see their heroes but they can't meet them.
6 At Comic Con you can try new video games.

6 **Word work** **Match the definitions to the words in bold in the text.**

1 people who draw or paint ________
2 someone who people admire ________
3 the clothes a person (e.g. an actor) wears to look like a different person ________
4 the signatures of famous people ________
5 very big ________
6 feeling very happy about something ________

7 **The words in bold are in the wrong sentence. Correct the sentences.**

1 An elephant is an **excited** animal.
2 Leonardo da Vinci was a famous **hero**.
3 Superman is my favorite comic book **artist**.
4 People wear special **autographs** for Carnival.
5 It's my birthday tomorrow – I'm really **enormous**!
6 Some people like collecting **costumes**.

CRITICAL THINKING — SUPER SKILLS

1 **Understand** Circle the correct sentence.
  a We use a live feed to report actions or events when they are happening.
  b We use a live feed to write about general information or things in the past.

2 **Apply** Which of these events could you describe using a live feed?
- the biography of a famous person
- a football game
- your last vacation
- an election
- an awards ceremony (Oscars, Grammys)

3 **Create** Think of two more events you could report with a live feed.

CELEBRITY CORNER

Sometimes actors, like Lupita Nyong'o, go to Comic Con in superhero costumes and people don't know it's them! Find other celebrities who go to Comic Con.

COMIC CON

Facts

Comic Con festivals are for people who like comic books, video games and movies.

Many countries have festivals for comic fans, including the USA, Brazil, the Philippines and India.

Fans often dress up as their favorite characters from science fiction and superhero movies.

3:31 pm

Now I'm in the Game Zone. It's the place to be for video game fans. Lots of fans are here and they're having a great time! They're playing this year's new games. More from Comic Con later!

2:47 pm

Comic Con is a great place to see actors, artists and other stars. A lot of fans are getting **autographs** and you can take a photo with your **hero**.

1:54 pm

I'm now in Artists' Alley. People are buying comic books and watching their favorite **artists** at work. What's this man doing? He's drawing a comic – it's really interesting to watch him draw.

12:32 pm

A man on the stage has a hat on and he's wearing striped blue tights. His face is completely white and his hair is orange! Another great costume – he's the Mad Hatter from *Alice in Wonderland*. Fantastic!

12:15 pm

I can see some amazing costumes. One man is wearing an **enormous** green top and brown pants – wait – he's turning around. He's the Hulk!

12:01 pm

The doors are opening now and hundreds of people are coming through the doors. The organizers are telling people to go slowly but the fans aren't listening. They all want to get in. So many people!

11:25 am

The day's just starting but already a lot of people are waiting to get in. Hundreds of Comic Con fans are arriving and some of them are wearing amazing **costumes**. Everyone's very **excited**.

Present progressive

1 **Read the examples. Complete the table with *aren't*, *isn't*, *listening*, *'m* or *'s*.**

People **are buying** comic books.
He**'s wearing** striped blue tights.
The fans **aren't listening**.

Affirmative/Negative		
subject	***be***	**verb *-ing***
I	1	buying ... wearing ...
You/We/They	're	
He/She/It	2	
subject	***be + not***	**verb *-ing***
I	'm not	5
You/We/They	3	
He/She/It	4	

2 **Read the Spelling rules on p45. Complete the sentences with the present progressive form of the verbs in parentheses.**

1 They ________ **(take)** photos.
2 I ________ **(play)** a video game.
3 You ________ **(not wear)** a costume.
4 He ________ **(wait)** to get an autograph.
5 She ________ **(not sit)** in the café.

3 **Write sentences that are true for you. Use the present progressive.**

1 I *'m sitting in class. I'm not wearing a hat.*
2 My teacher ________________
3 My classmates and I ________________
4 The person next to me ________________

4 **Copy the tables. Add the examples in the box.**

What**'s** this man **doing**? Drawing a comic.
Are they **having** a good time? Yes, they **are**.
Is he **wearing** a costume? No, he **isn't**.

***Wh-* questions**			
question word	***be***	**subject**	**verb *-ing***
Where	are	they	going?

***Yes/No* questions and short answers**			
be	**subject**	**verb *-ing***	
Am	I	sitting	in your chair?
Yes/No,	**subject**	***be (+ not)***	
No,	you	aren't.	

5 **Complete the text message conversation. Write sentences in the present progressive.**

MIA **1** you / do / homework / ? 3:50
2 No / I / not. 3:52 LUKE
MIA **3** What / you / do? 3:54
4 I / play / a video game. 3:55 LUKE
5 you / watch / soccer? 3:56 LUKE
MIA **6** Yes / I. Cruz Azul is playing really well! 3:58
MIA **7** They / win 3–1. 3:59

6 **Practice the conversation in exercise 5 with a partner.**

7 **Answer the question to solve the Brain teaser.**

BRAIN TEASER

Write sentences to describe all the problems you can see.

What is wrong in this picture?

Pronunciation: /n/ and /ŋ/ p128
Reinforcement and Challenge Grammar bootcamp p120

Describing clothes

1 Match descriptions 1–8 with photos A–H.

2 Match adjectives 1–7 with opposites a–g.

1 dressy
2 thick
3 long
4 baggy
5 comfortable
6 trendy
7 expensive

a tight
b uncomfortable
c casual
d old-fashioned
e cheap
f thin
g short

3 Work in pairs. Ask questions about clothes using adjectives.

Do you prefer casual clothes or dressy clothes?

I prefer casual clothes. Do you like baggy jeans?

A live report

FUN FACTS

Many schools with a uniform have a 'No Uniform Day'. Students pay £1 or $1 to wear their own clothes. Schools use the money for a party or a trip, or they give it to charity.

4 21 Listen to a reporter for a school radio station. Do the students like No Uniform Day?

1 Ella: yes/no
2 Dylan: yes/no
3 Kate: yes/no

Subskill: Listening to questions and answers

In live reports, listen carefully to the questions that the interviewer asks, as well as the answers.

5 Listen again. Complete the table.

	What is he/she wearing today?
Ella	
Dylan	
Kate	

6 Listen again. Complete the sentences with adjectives.

1 Andy thinks Ella's clothes are very ________ .
2 Dylan is wearing ________ clothes today.
3 Dylan thinks it's crazy to buy ________ clothes for No Uniform Day.
4 Kate thinks her school uniform is ________ and ________ .

7 Work in pairs. What are the advantages and disadvantages of school uniforms? Do you think they're a good idea?

Simple present and present progressive

1 **Read the examples in the table and circle the correct option to complete the rules.**

Simple present	Present progressive
My friend **goes** to a different school.	People **are arriving**.
He **doesn't wear** a school uniform.	I**'m not wearing** trendy clothes.
Do you **like** No Uniform Day?	What**'s** he **wearing**?

1 We use the **simple present/present progressive** to talk about actions that are in progress now.
2 We use the **simple present/present progressive** to talk about routines or habits.

We don't use the present progressive with some verbs, e.g. *be*, *like*, *love*, *want*.

2 **Circle the correct option.**

1 At the moment, I **wear/'m wearing** a coat.
2 We **don't go/aren't going** to school on Saturdays.
3 It **doesn't rain/isn't raining** today.
4 **Are you wearing/Do you wear** the same shoes every day?

Time expressions

3 **Copy and complete the table with the time expressions in the box.**

~~at the moment~~ every day every Monday now ~~on Saturdays~~ right now sometimes this week today usually

Simple present	Present progressive
on Saturdays	*at the moment*

4 **Complete the sentences with the simple present or present progressive form of the verbs in parentheses.**

1 'Can I borrow your dictionary?'
'Sorry, I (...) **(use)** it right now.'
2 'What (...) **(Sam / read)** ?'
'It's probably a comic book. He (...) **(usually / read)** comic books.'
3 '(...) **(your teacher / give)** you lots of homework?'
'Not usually, but today we (...) **(study)** for a test.'
4 'Alice (...) **(not sit)** in her usual place.'
'No, she (...) **(talk)** to Kim about their project.'

5 **Write questions in the simple present or present progressive.**

1 What / you / do / in the evenings ?
2 What / other people in your family / do / now ?
3 What / you / usually / wear / to go out ?
4 What / your teacher / wear / today ?
5 What language / you / speak / at home ?

6 **Work in pairs. Ask and answer the questions in exercise 5.**

7 **Circle the correct option.**

GRAMMAR ROUND-UP
1 2 3 4 5 6 7 8

Teenager sells a MILLION dollars ... in socks!

It's seven o'clock in the evening. Most kids **1** (...) now, but not high-school student Brennan Agranoff. He **2** (...) new designs for socks.

Brennan **3** (...) about six hours every day on his business. He **4** (...) a computer to make interesting designs and then prints **5** (...) on socks. Then he sells the socks online.

Why **6** (...) he do it? Well, people **7** (...) socks in one color, and he thinks that that's boring. He loves **8** (...) things and he also wants to be an entrepreneur.

Brennan **9** (...) more than 500 designs for socks now, but he plans to create more in the future.

	a	b	c
1	**a** relax	**b** is relaxing	**c** are relaxing
2	**a** create	**b** is creating	**c** are creating
3	**a** spend	**b** spends	**c** is spending
4	**a** uses	**b** is using	**c** use
5	**a** it	**b** they	**c** them
6	**a** is	**b** does	**c** do
7	**a** usually wear	**b** wear usually	**c** usually wearing
8	**a** make	**b** makes	**c** making
9	**a** is	**b** has	**c** have

Reinforcement and Challenge Grammar bootcamp p121

Shopping for clothes

1 **Work in pairs. Ask and answer the questions.**

1 Do you like shopping for clothes?
2 What are your favorite clothing stores?
3 Who do you usually go shopping with?

2 **Watch the video. What does Archie buy?**

3 **Read the Key phrases. Who says them, the shop assistant or the customer?**

4 **Watch again. Which Key phrases do you hear?**

5 **Complete the dialogue with the Key phrases. Watch again and check.**

Shop assistant: Hi! Do you need any help?

Archie: Oh, I'm **1** ________ a sweater. I like the colour of this one. **2** ________ is it?

Shop assistant: It's £25.

Archie: Can I **3** ________ , please?

Shop assistant: Sure, the changing rooms are over there.

Archie: Thank you! Excuse me, it's a bit small. **4** ________ is it?

Shop assistant: Hold on. It's a small.

Archie: Have you got this **5** ________ ?

Shop assistant: Here you go. It looks good.

Archie: OK, **6** ________ .

6 **Create your own dialogue. Follow the steps in the Skills boost.**

SKILLS BOOST

THINK
Look at the photos and choose one thing to buy.

PREPARE
Prepare a dialogue. Use the Key phrases.

PRACTICE
Practice your dialogue. Take turns being the customer.

PERFORM
Act out your dialogue for the class.

7 **Peer review** **Listen to your classmates and answer the questions.**

1 What clothes do your classmates buy?
2 Do they use the Key phrases correctly?

Key phrases

Do you need any help?
I'm/We're just looking, thanks.
I'm looking for (a sweater/some jeans).
How much is it/are they?
Can I try it/them on, please?
The changing rooms are over there.
It's/They're a bit (small/big/tight/baggy).
What size is it/are they?
Have you got this/these in a (small/medium/large)?
I'll take it/them.

UK → US

colour (UK) → color (US)
shop assistant (UK) → salesperson (US)

Selfie time

Do you like taking selfies? We want to see them!
Write a description of your favorite selfies and tell us why you like them …

A

In this photo, I'm standing in front of a blue door. I'm wearing a yellow top, a blue shirt and a hat. I always wear hats! I have the camera in front of me, so you can't see my face. You can only see my face on the screen. I love taking selfies and I like this photo because it's interesting and funny.

B

This is a photo of me with my friends. We don't go to the same school, so we only meet on weekends. We're sitting in front of my house. Jack's wearing jeans and red sneakers. Ali's wearing a yellow sweater. Laura's wearing a jacket and green glasses. I'm wearing a T-shirt, pants and a blue hat. I like this photo because we're having fun.

Photo descriptions

1 **Describe the photos. Which photo do you prefer? Why?**

2 **Read the selfie descriptions. Why does the writer like each photo?**

3 **Answer the questions for each photo.**

1 Where are the people?

____

2 What clothes is each person wearing?

____

▶ Subskill: *because* and *so*

We use *because* and *so* to connect ideas in a sentence. We use them when we give a reason or talk about a result.

4 **Find two examples of *because* and two examples of *so* in the selfie descriptions. Circle the correct option in the rules.**

1 We use ***because*/*so*** to give a reason.

2 We use ***because*/*so*** to talk about a result.

5 **Complete the sentences with *because* or *so*.**

1 It's my birthday _________ we're having a special dinner.

2 I'm wearing my uniform _________ I'm walking home from school.

3 I'm not going to school today _________ I'm sick.

4 It's really cold _________ I'm wearing a coat and hat.

5 I'm in my room _________ I'm doing my homework.

6 **Complete the sentences with your own ideas.**

1 We don't have school today because __________

____

2 I don't like sports so __________

____

3 It's hot today so __________

____

4 I hardly ever go to the movies because __________

____

5 I love photography so __________

____

7 **Write descriptions of two of your selfies. Follow the steps in the Skills boost.**

SKILLS BOOST

THINK

1 Choose two selfies.

2 Make notes about the photos. Use questions a–f to help you.

- **a** Where are you? ______
- **b** Why are you there? ______
- **c** What are you wearing? ______
- **d** Who are you with? ______
- **e** What are they doing/wearing? ______
- **f** Why do you like the photo? ______

PREPARE

Choose which questions to answer and decide the order of information a–f.

Photo A: ______

Photo B: ______

WRITE

Write your descriptions.

In this photo, I'm sitting in my room ...

I'm wearing ...

I like this photo because ...

CHECK

Read your descriptions and answer the questions.

1 Do you use the present progressive to describe the photos? ☐

2 Do you use the simple present to talk about habits and routines? ☐

3 Do you use *because* and *so* correctly? ☐

8 **Peer review** **Exchange your descriptions with another student. Which of the descriptions do you prefer? Why?**

Quick review

Grammar

Present progressive

Affirmative and negative

be (+ *not*) + verb *-ing*

*I'**m (am) reading** my favorite comic book.*

*He **isn't (is not) taking** photos.*

Questions and short answers

(Question word) + *be* + subject + verb *-ing*

*What**'s (is)** she **wearing**?* *A coat.*

***Are** they **having** a good time? Yes, they **are**./No, they **aren't**.*

We don't use the contracted form in affirmative short answers.

✓ Yes, they are. ~~Yes, they're.~~

✓ Yes, I am. ~~Yes, I'm.~~

Spelling rules

Most verbs: + *-ing* *buy → buying*

Verbs which end in *-e*: remove *e* + *-ing* *take → taking*

Some verbs which end in consonant + vowel + consonant: double consonant + *-ing* *swim → swimming*

Simple present and present progressive

We use the simple present to talk about routines or habits.

We use the present progressive to talk about actions that are in progress now.

Simple present	Present progressive
*We usually **wear** a school uniform.*	*We **are wearing** regular clothes today.*
*He **doesn't play** football on Wednesdays.*	*He **isn't playing** football today.*
***Do** you **have** lunch at school?* *Yes, I **do**./No, I **don't**.*	***Are** you **having** lunch?* *Yes, I **am**./No, I**'m not**.*
*What **does** he always **do**?*	*What **is** he **doing** now?*

Time expressions

With simple present:

always, sometimes, never, etc., every day/week/month/year, on Mondays/Tuesdays, etc., on weekends

With present progressive:

now, right now, at the moment, today, this morning/afternoon/evening, this week/month/year

Vocabulary

22 Clothes and accessories

boots, coat, dress, hat, hoodie, jacket, jeans, leggings, pants, sandals, scarf, shirt, shoes, shorts, skirt, sneakers, sunglasses, sweater, T-shirt, tights, top

23 Describing clothes

baggy, casual, cheap, comfortable, dressy, expensive, long, old-fashioned, short, thick, thin, tight, trendy, uncomfortable

3 Project

WDYT?
(What do you think?)

Why do people dress up?

TASK: Make a mini-book about traditional clothes.

Learning outcomes

1 I can describe traditional clothes from another country or region.

2 I can use my imagination to present information in an attractive way.

3 I can use appropriate language from the unit.

Graphic organizer → Project planner p132

1 Watch a video of a student making a mini-book. What do you need to make one?

STEP 1: THINK

2 Read the page from a mini-book in the Model project. Which of these things can you see?

- a title
- information about the country or region
- a description of the clothes
- information about when people wear these clothes
- an attractive picture of the costume
- information about the history of the region

STEP 2: PLAN

3 Work in pairs. Choose a region of your country, or another country.

4 Make notes about the following:

- Where is the region or country?
- What are the traditional clothes for men and for women?
- When do people wear these clothes?

5 Find one or more photos or draw a picture of the traditional clothes.

STEP 3: CREATE

6 Work in pairs. Read the tips in the Super skills box and practice saying the Key phrases with a partner.

CREATIVITY — SUPER SKILLS

Using your imagination and thinking of original ideas

Tips

Think of different ideas.

Try different options.

Decide what looks best.

Key phrases

What about ... ?

What do you think about ... ?

We could (write the title in red/put the picture here ...)

That's a good idea.

Mmm, I'm not sure.

That looks/doesn't look good.

7 Read the *How to ...* tips on p131. Then make your mini-book. Use the tips and Key phrases in the Super skills box.

Model project

Traditional costumes in BOLIVIA

Different regions of Bolivia have different costumes. Traditional clothes often tell us what region someone comes from.

The Highlands are a region in the west of Bolivia. The traditional costume there has a lot of colors. People wear it for festivals and on special occasions.

Men usually wear a red jacket, a white shirt, white pants and white shoes. They often wear a hat.

Women have very colorful costumes. They wear long pink, yellow or blue skirts and a hat, and they sometimes wear boots.

In these photos, men are playing instruments and women are dancing in the street during the Laja Festival in La Paz. They are wearing traditional clothes.

STEP 4: PRESENT

8 Peer review **Exchange your mini-book with another pair. As you read, answer the questions.**

1. What new things do you learn about traditional clothes?
2. Does the mini-book have information about the country/region and the clothes?
3. Is the mini-book attractive? Why/Why not?

3 FINAL REFLECTION

1 The task

Does your mini-book describe the region and clothes?

What details do you include?

2 Super skill

How interesting and attractive is your mini-book? Give examples.

3 Language

Do you use language from the unit? Give examples.

4 Extremes

WDYT?
(What do you think?)

How does the weather affect the way we live?

Vocabulary: seasons and weather; compound nouns: things to take on a trip

Grammar: comparative and superlative adjectives; modal verbs of obligation, permission and prohibition

Reading: a magazine article about extreme places to live

Listening: instructions for an adventure vacation in Yosemite

Speaking: making and responding to suggestions

Writing: instructions

Project: give weather advice to visitors to your country

Video skills p49

Real-world speaking p55

Project pp58–59

Seasons and weather

1 Write the words in the box in the correct category.

cold cool fall ~~hot~~ ~~rain~~ snow ~~spring~~ summer sun warm winter

Four seasons: *spring* ________

Four adjectives to describe temperature: *hot* ________

Three words to talk about the weather: *rain* ________

2 Work in pairs. Which is your favorite season? Why?

3 Look at the weather map. Match words 1–6 with definitions a–f.

1 ice	a short periods of rain
2 freezing	b with a lot of rain
3 wet	c with little or no rain
4 thunderstorm	d very, very cold
5 showers	e water that is solid because it's cold
6 dry	f violent weather

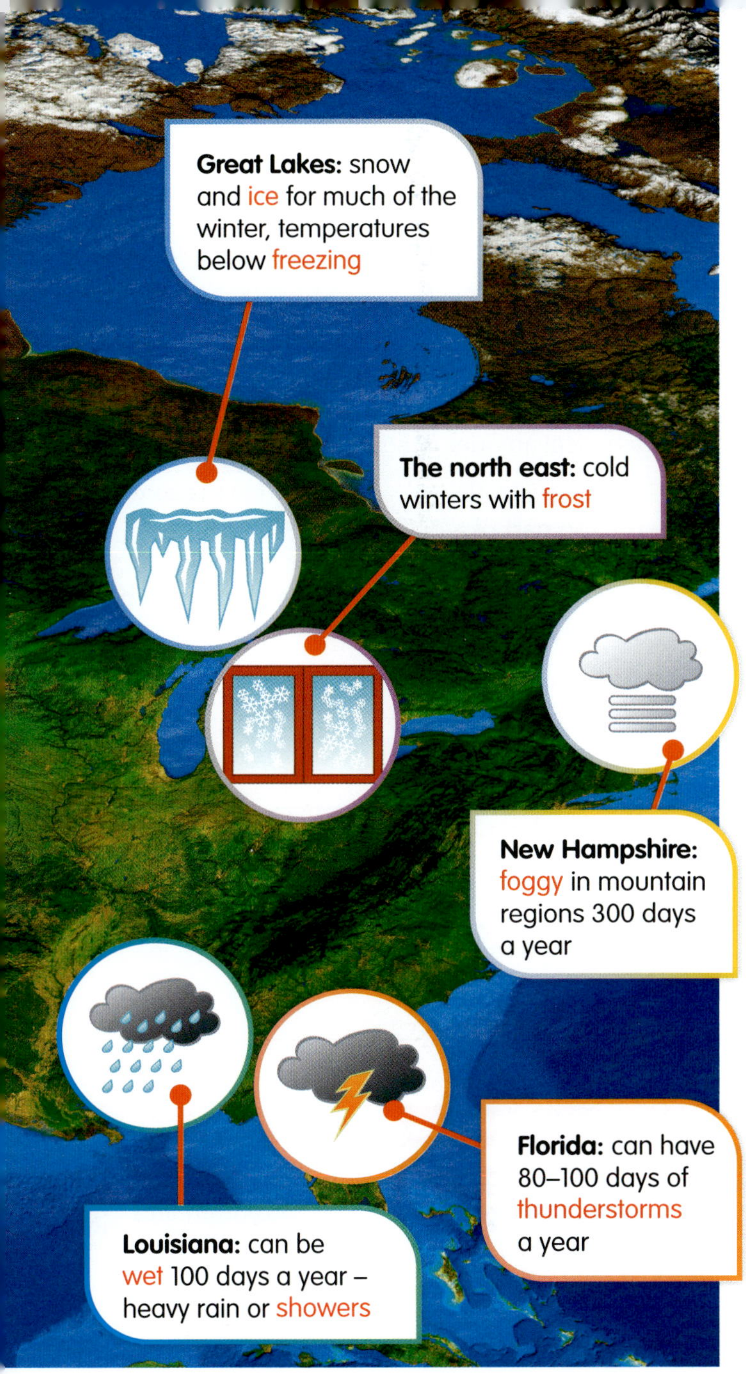

4 **Complete the table. What letter do we often add to make adjectives?**

Noun	Adjective
1	icy
sun	2
cloud	3
4	windy
fog	5
6	frosty

5 **How do you say the words in exercise 4 in your language?**

6 24 **Listen. What words can you use to describe the weather?**

7 **Circle the correct option.**

In Phoenix, Arizona, it's never cold. In the spring and fall it's warm and **1 sun/sunny**, and in the summer it's really hot! It hardly ever **2 rain/rains**, it's usually **3 wet/dry**.

In New York, winters are cold and **4 ice/icy**. Sometimes there is **5 frost/frosty** at night in November and April. In the spring, it's often **6 cloud/cloudy**. Summers are hot with the occasional thunderstorm. Fall is cool and sometimes **7 fog/foggy**.

8 **Work in pairs and answer the questions.**

1 What's the weather like where you live ... ?
  - **a** in the spring
  - **b** in the summer
  - **c** in the fall
  - **d** in the winter

2 What's the weather like in the north, south, east, west of your country?

3 What's the weather like today?

VIDEO SKILLS

9 **Watch the video and answer the questions.**

1 Why is the video called 'Four seasons in a week'?

2 What things do you need to be ready for the weather in the UK?

10 **Work in pairs. Discuss the questions.**

1 What do you learn about in the video?

2 What more would you like to know?

3 Why is video a good way to learn about the weather?

A magazine article

1 **Look at the photos and read the fact files. What is the weather like in Mawsynram and Oymyakon?**

2 **Match each word with Mawsynram or Oymyakon. Use a dictionary to help you.**

bridge freeze reindeer roots umbrella

Subskill: Understanding the main idea

The first time you read a text, read it quickly to get a general idea of what it is about.

3 **Read the magazine article quickly. What is it about? Circle the correct option.**

a Weather disasters around the world
b How the world's weather is changing
c Living in extreme weather conditions

4 25 **Read and listen to the text. Answer the questions.**

1 When does it rain every day in Mawsynram?
2 What do people put over their heads when it rains?
3 Why do they make bridges from trees?
4 What happens to cell phones in Oymyakon?
5 What do people eat there? Why?
6 When do schools close?

5 **Are the sentences true for Mawsynram, Oymyakon or both?**

1 People usually stay at home in extreme weather.
2 In some months of the year, it's difficult to sleep.
3 The days are very short here.
4 People use plants and trees to help them.
5 The town is a long way from a big city.
6 People learn to live with extreme weather.

6 **Word work** **Match the definitions to the words in bold in the text.**

1 a loud sound ______
2 breaks completely ______
3 a type of plant – it grows in a yard or park ______
4 a typical amount of something ______
5 continue to exist ______
6 the top part of a building ______

7 **Complete the sentences with the words in bold in the text.**

1 You can usually see birds on the ______ of our house.
2 My ______ grade at school is 8.5.
3 What's that ______ ? Are you having a party?
4 Classes at my school ______ 45 minutes.
5 Amy's sitting on the ______ in the yard.
6 A tropical storm ______ houses and roads.

CRITICAL THINKING **SUPER SKILLS**

1 **Remember** List the things that are difficult for the people of Mawsynram and Oymyakon.
2 **Analyze** Order the things from most difficult to least difficult in each place.
3 **Evaluate** Decide which is the more difficult place to live in. Think about:

clothes daily routines food and drink free-time activities houses transportation

Research

Find out what the average temperature and rainfall are where you live.

OUR AMAZING WORLD

Today we're looking at extreme weather in two very different places.

Fact file
MAWSYNRAM
Location: north-west India
Population: 237 families
Average rainfall: 11,871 mm

Let's start with Mawsynram in India. It isn't cold there, but it is wet. This is the wettest place in the world. The monsoon season is longer here than in any other place, and it rains every day!

The heaviest rain is at night, so people put **grass** on the walls and **roof** of their homes to stop the **noise**.

They stay at home most of the time in the rainy season. When they go out, they carry bamboo umbrellas over their heads.

They use the roots of living trees to make bridges across rivers. Students use these when they walk to school. The rain **destroys** regular bridges, but these living bridges can **last** for hundreds of years.

Fact file
OYMYAKON
Location: north-east Russia
Population: 500
Lowest temperature: -71.2°C

In the winter, Oymyakon in Siberia is the coldest town in the world. The **average** temperature is -50°C, and it's dark for 21 hours of the day.

Life here isn't easy. People can only stay outside for a minute or two, and they can't make a phone call in the street because cell phones freeze!

Vegetables don't grow here, so people usually eat meat and drink reindeer milk. They hardly ever go shopping because the nearest city is two days away by car.

In other countries, students don't go to school when it snows, but in Oymyakon, snow and ice are normal. Here, schools only close when the temperature is lower than -52°C!

Life in Mawsynram and Oymyakon is more difficult than in other places, but the people of these two towns find ways to live with extreme weather every day.

Comparative and superlative adjectives

1 Read the examples. Which sentences compare two things? Which compare three or more things?

Siberia is **colder** than India.
This is the **coldest** town in the world.
India is **wetter** than Siberia.
May and June are the **wettest** months.

2 Read the sentences again. Complete the rules.

1 To compare two things, use comparative adjective + ________ .
2 To compare three or more things, use ________ + superlative adjective.

3 Read the Spelling rules on p57. Complete the table.

Adjective	Comparative	Superlative
cold	**colder**	1
wet	2	**wettest**
heavy	3	**heaviest**
difficult	**more difficult**	4
good	**better**	**best**
bad	**worse**	5

4 Complete the sentences with comparative adjectives.

1 India is ________ **(hot)** than the UK.
2 Perth is ________ **(windy)** than Chicago.
3 The Antarctic is ________ **(cold)** than the Arctic.
4 Snow is ________ **(good)** than ice for skiing.
5 Thunderstorms are ________ **(dangerous)** than showers.

5 Write sentences about Brazil and Ecuador with comparative adjectives.

1 Brazil / big / Ecuador
____
2 Quito / high / Brasilia
____
3 Summers in Brasilia / hot / in Quito
____
4 Winters in Quito / cool / in Brasilia
____
5 Quito / wet / Brasilia
____

CELEBRITY CORNER

Actor **Jessica Biel** climbed the highest mountain in Africa for charity. Which mountain is it?

6 Complete the quiz questions with superlative adjectives. Then listen and check.

WORLD RECORDS

1 Which is *the highest* **(high)** mountain?
a K2 b Lhotse c Everest

2 Which is ________ **(small)** country?
a Andorra b Vatican city c Monaco

3 Which is ________ **(hot)** place?
a Tunisia b California c India

4 Which is ________ **(popular)** country for tourists?
a Spain b Thailand c France

5 Which is ________ **(dry)** desert?
a the Atacama b the Sahara c the Arabian

6 Which is ________ **(big)** ocean?
a the Indian Ocean b the Atlantic c the Pacific

7 26 Circle the correct answers in the quiz. Listen and check.

8 Complete the text with the comparative or superlative form of the adjectives in parentheses.

Dubai has more world records than any other place. The **1** (...) **(tall)** hotel in the world is here, and the **2** (...) **(big)** shopping center. The IMG Worlds of Adventure theme park is **3** (...) **(large)** than any other theme park. It has some of the **4** (...) **(exciting)** rides in the world!

People often think that Dubai is **5** (...) **(expensive)** than other cities, but in fact many things are **6** (...) **(cheap)**. Many tourists come here every year and the airport is now **7** (...) **(busy)** than London's Heathrow!

9 Answer the question to solve the Brain teaser.

BRAIN TEASER

Antalya and Izmir are two of the hottest places in Turkey. In Antalya, the highest average temperature in July is 34°C. In Istanbul, it's five degrees lower. Rize is one of the coolest places in July. The average temperature there is three degrees lower than in Istanbul.

What's the average temperature in Rize in July?

Reinforcement and Challenge Grammar bootcamp p121

Compound nouns: things to take on a trip

1 **Read the brochure and answer the questions.**

1 What is Outward Bound?
2 What type of activities do they organize?
3 What do people learn through these activities?

The Outward Bound organization offers outdoor education programs for young people and adults in over 30 countries. Courses last from two days to several months and can include canoeing, climbing and camping.

On this one-week expedition, middle school students walk, cook and spend time in beautiful Yosemite National Park. Teamwork and communication are two of the most important things you learn.

Things you need:
- backpack
- sleeping bag
- water bottle
- pocketknife

2 **Write a list of clothes to take on an Outward Bound trip.**

3 **Read the list of things you need in the brochure. Can you find them in the photos?**

4 **Complete the table using words from the box to make compound nouns.**

bag (x2) book (x2) bottle brush (x2) case screen knife jacket ~~pack~~ paste ~~towel~~

One word	
back*pack*	hair_________
guide_________	pocket_________
suit_________	tooth_________
tooth_________	sun_________
Two words	
beach *towel*	waterproof _________
sleeping _________	phrase _________
toiletry _________	water _________

5 **Match the photos in exercise 3 with the items in the table.**

6 **Work in pairs. Which other things would you take on a trip to Yosemite?**

Instructions

Subskill: Using pictures to help you understand

Before you listen, look at the pictures. Can you name them? What other words could you hear? E.g. *camera: take photos*

7 27 **Listen to a guide at Yosemite Park. Order the pictures.**

a	b	c	d	e	f	g

8 **Listen again and complete the rules.**

1 Please listen to the guides at all _________ .
2 You can take _________ but not _________ .
3 Never give food to any _________ .
4 Don't leave any food in your _________ .
5 Put your toothpaste in a special _________ .
6 It's very sunny and hot so wear a _________ and bring sunscreen and a _________ .

9 **Work in pairs. Would you like to go on a trip like this? Talk about the advantages and disadvantages.**

Modal verbs of obligation, permission and prohibition

1 **Read the examples. Complete the table with *can*, *can't*, *must* and *mustn't*.**

You **can** take photos.
You **can't** leave any food in your backpack.
Can we take food into the park? Yes, you **can**.
Can we give food to the animals? No, you **can't**.
All food **must** go in these special boxes.
You **mustn't** take any plants or flowers with you.

Obligation	Permission	Prohibition
1	2	3 4

2 **Complete the tables with the examples in exercise 1.**

Affirmative and negative			
subject	***can/can't/ must/mustn't***	**verb**	
You	**can**	take	photos.
1			
2			
You	**mustn't**	take	any plants.

Questions and short answers			
Can	**subject**	**verb**	
Can	we	take	food into the park?
3			
Yes/No	**subject**	***can/can't***	
Yes,	you	**can**.	
4			

3 **Rewrite the sentences using the words and symbols in parentheses.**

1 You can take photos. **(we / ?)**
Can we take photos?
2 You must bring a small backpack. **(you / -)**
3 You can call home on weekends. **(I / ?)**
4 Can we drink the water here? **(you / -)**
5 Can we wear shorts today? **(we / +)**
6 We mustn't eat here. **(you / +)**
7 You can't wear sneakers for this walk. **(we / ?)**

4 **Rewrite the rules using *can*, *can't*, *must* and *mustn't*.**

1 It's OK to bring your bike. *You can bring your bike.*
2 It's OK to come in a group of up to eight people.
3 It's very important to come with an adult.
4 It's important that you don't stay overnight.
5 It's OK to visit from March through November.
6 It's important to wear shoes, not sandals.

5 **Read the school rules and rewrite them so they are true for your school.**

1 You can use your cell phone in class.
2 You must run in the school building.
3 You can't use a ball in the playground.
4 You can wear your own clothes.
5 You mustn't arrive before 9:00.
6 You can eat and drink in the classroom.

6 **Circle the correct option.**

GRAMMAR ROUND-UP

1 2 3 4 5 6 7 8

My family and I **1 go sometimes/sometimes go** on vacation in the Sierra de Guara. It's a beautiful place, but I love **2 it/him** because it's the **3 best/better** place I know to go canyoning.

Canyoning is a fantastic sport to do in the spring or summer. First you walk up a mountain with your guide. That's quite difficult because **4 you wearing/you are wearing** a wetsuit! Then you go down the mountain, but it's **5 harder/more hard** than it sounds because you walk in a river! I think canyoning is **6 interesting/more interesting** than other sports because it's a mix of swimming, jumping from rocks and climbing.

If you're very good, you **7 can go/can to go** alone, but **8 we always go/we go always** with a group. Canyoning is a lot of fun but you **9 must listen/can listen** to the guide because it can be dangerous.

Research

Can you go canyoning near where you live?

Pronunciation: *can* p128

Reinforcement and Challenge Grammar bootcamp p122

Making and responding to suggestions

1 **Look at the photo. Is there a park like this near where you live?**

2 **Watch the video. Is it a school trip or are the friends organizing it?**

3 **Complete the dialogue with the Key phrases. Watch again and check.**

Kirsty: I'm really excited about our day out tomorrow.

Sam: Me, too. What time does the zip line open?

Kirsty: Ummm – 8:00. So I think we **1** ________ get the bus at 8:30.

Sam: Really? That's too early! How **2** ________ the 9:00 bus?

Kirsty: OK, **3** ________ .

Sam: Do we need special clothes?

Kirsty: Ummm – comfortable clothes, sneakers, but you can't wear sandals.

Sam: What about lunch?

Kirsty: Why **4** ________ take a picnic? It'll be cheaper that way.

Sam: Yes, **5** ________ . Oh, this looks awesome. It has the longest zip lines in California!

Kirsty: Look, this one's 2,700 feet long!

Sam: Amazing!

4 **Create your own dialogue. Follow the steps in the Skills boost.**

SKILLS BOOST

THINK
Think of a place to visit (e.g. a theme park, water park, a stadium...)
Make notes about times, price, travel, food and clothes/things you need.

PREPARE
Prepare a dialogue to discuss options for your trip. Remember to include Key phrases for making and responding to suggestions.

PRACTICE
Practice your dialogue.

PERFORM
Act out your dialogue for the class.

5 **Peer review** **Listen to your classmates and answer the questions.**

1 Where do they choose to visit?
2 Which Key phrases do they use?

Key phrases

Making suggestions: We should (go by train).
Let's (get the bus).
Why don't we (take a picnic)?
How about (getting the 9:00 bus)?
Agreeing with suggestions: OK, fine.
Good idea.
Disagreeing with suggestions: Really? That's too early.
I'm not sure. I don't like (picnics).

US → UK

sneakers (US) → trainers (UK)
This looks awesome! (US) → This looks brilliant! (UK)

Get it right: HOW TO PACK FOR A CAMPING TRIP

1 When you go on a camping vacation, it's important to pack your backpack well. It's easier to carry the heavier things at the top. The lighter things go at the bottom of the backpack.

2 The top of your backpack is for things you need while traveling. This is a good place for your hat, your water bottle and a snack too. The top section also has space to put your waterproof jacket: it's easy to get it out if it starts to rain.

3 The bottom section is the biggest and this is where you pack the things you don't need while you are traveling to the campsite. Your sleeping bag is probably the biggest thing you're carrying, but it's also quite light. It's a good idea to pack this first, right at the bottom. After that, pack your clothes, cooking equipment and the rest of your food too.

Instructions

1 Look at the diagram and read the packing instructions. Order the paragraphs.

a The top section

b Introduction and general information

c The bottom of the backpack

2 Complete the table with the things you pack in each section and why.

	What?	Why?
top		
bottom		

a sleeping bag

b water bottle and waterproof jacket

c clothes and cooking equipment

d because you don't need them during the day

e because it's big but light

f because you use these things while traveling

▶ Subskill: *too* and *also*

To add another idea, use words like *too* and *also*.

3 Find two sentences with *too* and two sentences with *also* in the text. Complete the rules with *too* and *also*.

1 ________ comes at the end of sentences with a list.

2 ________ comes after the verb *be* and before other verbs.

4 Rewrite the sentences with *too* and *also* in the correct position.

1 I normally pack a waterproof jacket and waterproof pants. **(too)**

2 I like surfing and I like going on zip lines. **(also)**

3 We go to Italy on vacation and to see my grandparents. **(too)**

4 My suitcase is very big. It's very heavy. **(also)**

5 I listen to music on my cell phone and I take photos with it. **(also)**

6 The sun's very hot today. You must wear a hat and sunscreen. **(too)**

5 Write instructions for how to pack for a beach vacation. You can take a small bag for the trip (carry-on bag) and a suitcase. Follow the steps in the Skills boost.

SKILLS BOOST

THINK

1 Think of things to take on a beach vacation. Divide them into two groups:

Carry-on bag	Suitcase
cell phone	*shorts*

2 Compare with a partner. Is anything missing?

3 Write sentences about packing these things. Use the information in exercise 1 and the underlined phrases from the text.

It's important to put your cell phone in your carry-on bag.

PREPARE

Organize your notes into paragraphs:

Paragraph 1: general introduction

Paragraph 2: suitcase

Paragraph 3: carry-on bag

WRITE

Write your instructions. Use the example in exercise 1 to help you.

When you go on a beach vacation it's important to pack your suitcase and carry-on bag well.

CHECK

Read your instructions. Answer the questions.

1 Do you use *also* and *too* correctly? ☐

2 Do you use comparatives and superlatives? ☐

3 Do you use modal verbs? ☐

6 Peer review Exchange your instructions with another student. Are the instructions clear and easy to understand? Is anything missing?

Quick review

Grammar

Comparatives and superlatives

To compare two things, use comparative adjective + *than*.
To compare three things, use *the* + superlative adjective.
Madrid is ***warmer than*** *Santander.*
Seville is ***the hottest*** *place in Spain.*

Spelling of comparative and superlative adjectives

One syllable adjectives → + *-er*, *-est*
If the adjective ends in -e → + *-r*, *-st*
*cold → cold**er** → the cold**est***
*white → white**r** → the white**st***
One syllable adjectives ending in vowel + consonant → double the final consonant + *-er*, *-est*
*hot → hot**ter** → the hot**test***
Adjectives ending in *-y* → ~~y~~ + *-ier*, *-iest*
*sunny → sunn**ier** → the sunn**iest***
Adjectives with two or more syllables → *more*, *the most* + adjective
beautiful → ***more*** *beautiful →* ***the most*** *beautiful*
Irregular
good → better → the best   *bad → worse → the worst*

Modal verbs of obligation, permission and prohibition

Use *can* to give/ask about permission.
You ***can*** *ask questions now.*
Can *we take photos?*   *Yes, you* ***can***.
Use *must* to talk about obligation.
You ***must*** *arrive at 9:00.*
Use *can't* and *mustn't* to talk about prohibition.
You ***can't*** *use a dictionary.*   *You* ***mustn't*** *eat in class.*

Affirmative and negative

Use subject + *can/can't/must/mustn't* + verb.
No change for *he/she/it*:
She can swim.

Questions and short answers

For questions, use *can* + subject + verb?
For short answers, use *Yes/No*, + subject + *can/can't*.

Vocabulary

28 Seasons and weather

Seasons: fall, spring, summer, winter
Temperature: cold, cool, freezing, hot, warm
Weather: cloud, cloudy, dry, fog, foggy, frost, frosty, ice, icy, rain, showers, snow, sun, sunny, thunderstorms, wet, wind, windy

29 Compound nouns: things to take on a trip

backpack, beach towel, guidebook, hairbrush, phrase book, pocketknife, sleeping bag, suitcase, sunscreen, toiletry bag, toothbrush, toothpaste, water bottle, waterproof jacket

4 Project

WDYT?
(What do you think?)

How does the weather affect the way we live?

TASK: Make a video giving weather advice to visitors to your country.

Learning outcomes

1 I can speak about the weather in my country.
2 I can listen when I work with other students.
3 I can use appropriate language from the unit.

Graphic organizer → Project planner p131

1 Watch a video of a student giving weather advice. Which seasons does she talk about?

STEP 1: THINK

2 Read the notes about Finland in the Model project and answer the questions.

1 What is the same and what is different from the video?
2 What information can you see about each season?

STEP 2: PLAN

3 Work in pairs. Read the tips in the Super skills box and practice saying the Key phrases with a partner.

COMMUNICATION — SUPER SKILLS

Active listening

Tips

Don't interrupt when your partner is speaking.

Listen to what your partner says.

Repeat what your partner says to check that you understand.

Key phrases

You go first.	*OK, let me check if I understand.*
So you think ...	*Can you explain about ... ?*
Sorry, can you say that again?	*What do you mean about ... ?*

4 Work in pairs. Choose a region of your country and make notes about the following (don't write complete sentences). Use the tips and Key phrases in the Super skills box.

- What is the weather like ... ?

  in the spring — in the summer
  in the fall — in the winter
- What do people do in each season?
- What is it a good idea to bring at each time of year?

STEP 3: CREATE

5 Read the *How to ...* tips on p131. Then decide who says what in your video.

6 Practice saying your part of the video using notes only.

7 Record your video.

Model project

FINLAND

Four different seasons – different but beautiful!

Winter:

December to March, -30°C – 0°C

freezing temperatures, snow

people go skiing, snowboarding, ice-skating

Bring: thick coat, scarf, hat, gloves, waterproof boots

Spring/Fall:

April to May and September to November, 2°C – 15°C

cool, often windy, sometimes rains

people love walking in countryside

Bring: walking boots, a waterproof jacket, jeans, sweaters, a backpack, a water bottle

Summer:

June to August, 1°C – 32°C

warm and sunny

people spend time outside – swimming, fishing, sitting in sun

Bring: shorts, T-shirts, sandals, sunglasses, sunscreen

STEP 4: PRESENT

8 Peer review **Show your video to other students. As you watch, answer the questions.**

1 Is the information clear and helpful?

2 When would you like to visit this region? Why?

4 FINAL REFLECTION

1 The task

Can you talk about the weather in your country?

Is the information in your video clear and helpful?

2 Super skill

How well can you listen to other students? How do you know?

3 Language

Do you use language from the unit? Give examples.

5 Must try!

WDYT?
(What do you think?)

What makes a town a good place to live in?

Vocabulary: food and drink; places in a town

Grammar: countable and uncountable nouns; *there is/are; Is/Are there ... ? how much/ many ... ?*

Reading: a guidebook about local food

Listening: an informal conversation about a visit to Buenos Aires

Speaking: asking for directions

Writing: a description of a place

Project: make a map for young people moving to live in your town

Video skills p61

Real-world speaking p67

Project pp70–71

Food and drink

1 Look at this photo-sharing app for food lovers. Choose the missing food in each text from the words in the box.

banana cheese chicken chocolate oil peas rice

2 Complete the table with the words in exercise 1.

Meat/Fish	Carbs	Dairy	Fruits	Vegetables	Desserts	Other

FUN FOOD FACTS

a ______ comes in more than 100 different shapes; two of the most popular are spaghetti and macaroni.

b Cows are not the only animals to produce ______ . You can also get it from sheep, camels and reindeer!

c The USA and Brazil are the biggest producers of ______ . That's why burgers are so popular there.

d ______ are similar to pasta. They are popular in China and Japan.

e It takes over 20 liters of milk to make a kilo of ______ .

f A lot of people cry when they cut ______ . Some people say it helps to cut them under water.

g ______ is a liquid you put on food. Examples are ketchup and mayonnaise.

h People use ______ like pepper, oregano and curry when cooking to make food taste better.

3 **Read the Fun food facts and complete the text with some of the words in the box.**

beef butter cake eggs fries grapes herbs and spices ice cream melon milk mushrooms noodles onions pasta sauce yogurt

4 **Add the words from exercise 3 to the table in exercise 2.**

5 **Work in pairs. Can you add any more food items to the table?**

6 **Work in pairs. Ask and answer the questions.**

1 What's your favorite food?

My favorite food is chocolate. What about you?

I love bananas! I have one every morning for breakfast.

2 What do you eat for a snack?
3 What food don't you like?
4 What food do you eat on your birthday?

7 **Say three ingredients you use when you make ...**

1 a cake

______

2 pizza

______

8 **Think of a popular dish in your country. What are the ingredients?**

VIDEO SKILLS

9 **Watch the video and answer the questions.**

1 What cake and drink does she make?
2 What are the ingredients?

10 **Work in pairs. Discuss the questions.**

1 Why do people make 'how to' videos?
2 Why is this kind of video popular?
3 What could you make a 'how to' video about?

Pronunciation: /i/ and /ɪ/ p129

A guidebook

1 🔊30 **Listen to the descriptions. Can you name the food?**

2 **Work in pairs. Look at the photos on p63. Describe one to your partner. Can he/she identify the photo?**

3 **Look at the flags. Can you name the country? Do you know any food from these countries?**

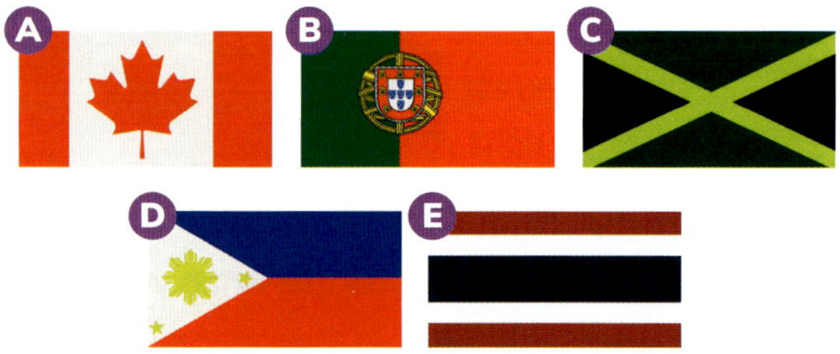

4 **Read the text quickly and name the food in the photos.**

Subskill: Identifying key words

To find specific information, you don't need to read the text in detail. Look over the text to identify the key words you need.

5 **Read the text quickly again. Complete the table.**

Dish	Country	Ingredients
poutine	1	2
3	Portugal	4
5	6	chicken, herbs and spices, rice, peas
halo-halo	7	8
pad Thai	9	eggs, noodles, beef, vegetables, chicken

6 🔊31 **Read and listen to the text in detail and correct the sentences.**

1 Poutine is a good thing to eat in the summer.
2 Pastel de nata is a delicious chocolate cake.
3 Jerk chicken and fries is popular in Jamaica.
4 Ice cream is the best thing on a hot day in the Philippines.
5 Pad Thai always has beef and chicken.

7 Word work **Match the definitions to the words in bold in the text.**

1 very tasty and good to eat ________
2 a combination of different things ________
3 something you notice with your nose ________
4 food you buy to eat somewhere else ________
5 put something extra ________
6 places (e.g. in a market) where you can buy food to eat in the street ________

8 **Complete the sentences with words from exercise 7.**

1 My dad's macaroni cheese is ________ .
2 My favorite ________ is pizza.
3 I hate the ________ of onions.
4 My favorite dish is a ________ of rice, vegetables and chicken.
5 To make ice cream even better, ________ chocolate sauce.
6 One of my favorite ________ sells pancakes with lemon and sugar.

9 **Work in pairs. Change the underlined words in exercise 8 so the sentences are true for you. Compare with your partner.**

10 **Work in pairs. Ask and answer the questions.**

1 What can you buy at food stands in your country?
2 Do you ever buy food to eat in the street?
3 What do you eat if you go out with your friends?

CRITICAL THINKING — SUPER SKILLS

1 **Remember** Which of the foods in the text would you like to try?
2 **Analyze** Put them in order from your favorite to least favorite
3 **Evaluate** What foreign food restaurants are there where you live?
4 Why should people try food from different places? Write a list of reasons.

Research

Choose a country and research a typical dish.

CELEBRITY CORNER

Celebrity chef **José Andrés'** charity helps give people food in times of need. What's the name of his charity?

HOW TO... EAT LIKE A LOCAL

When you visit other countries, forget fast food like burgers. There are some great local foods you must try. Here are some of our favorites!

If you're feeling cold and hungry in the winter in Canada, then there is only one thing to eat: poutine. There isn't a better snack! To make poutine, you take some fries, **add** some cheese and cover it all with gravy. It's a **delicious** way to get warm on a winter's day.

If you visit Portugal there is a fantastic cake you must eat called pastel de nata. It's a small cake made with eggs and butter. For me there's only one problem with pastel de nata: there isn't any chocolate!

Imagine: you're walking along the road in Kingston, Jamaica. Music is playing and there is a wonderful **smell** of herbs and spices. You're starting to feel really hungry and there's only one thing you want to eat: jerk chicken. There aren't any fries with this **takeout**. You eat jerk chicken with rice and peas.

The weather is tropical and it's sunny and hot. After a long day you want something cool and sweet. There are two alternatives. The first is ice cream. That sounds good, but in the Philippines there is something better: halo-halo. Halo-halo is a delicious **mix** of fruit, milk and lots more, but it's also beautiful and includes purple ice cream!

There are some great **food stands** in Thailand and one of the most popular dishes is pad Thai. The most important ingredients are eggs, noodles and vegetables, but you can add some beef or chicken if you like meat.

Countable and uncountable nouns

Some nouns are **countable**: we can count 1, 2, 3 eggs.

Some nouns are **uncountable**: we can't count water.

1 **Read the examples. Are the words in blue countable or uncountable nouns?**

It's a small **cake**.
I'd like some **fries**.
You eat it with **rice**.
Add some **beef**.
We have two **bananas**.
I can't see any **apples**.
We don't have any **milk**.

2 **Complete the table with the examples in exercise 1.**

Singular countable	
Affirmative	**Negative**
a/an + noun 1	–
Uncountable	
Affirmative	**Negative**
some + noun 2	*any* + noun 3
noun only You eat it with **rice**.	–
Plural	
Affirmative	**Negative**
some + noun 4	*any* + noun 5
number + noun We have two **bananas**.	–

3 32 **Read the interview with Jonah and circle the correct option. Listen and check.**

Paula: What do you have for breakfast?

Jonah: For breakfast I have **1 some/an** egg and **2 some/any** chocolate milk. I don't have **3 some/any** fruit in the morning.

Paula: What about lunch? Do you eat at school?

Jonah: Yes, I do. I usually have **4 –/a** pasta and **5 some/any** vegetables. Then, I normally have **6 a/an** apple or **7 a/some** grapes.

Paula: And in the evening?

Jonah: I usually have vegetables with **8 a/–** rice or **9 a/any** veggie burger. I don't eat **10 a/any** meat or fish. I'm a vegetarian.

4 **Work in pairs. Write your own answers to the interviewer's questions. Then compare your answers.**

there is/are

5 **Read the sentences, then complete the table.**

	Affirmative	**Negative**
Singular noun	**There is** a wonderful **smell**. *There* **1** ________ *a/an* + noun	**There isn't** a better **snack**. *There* **2** ________ *a /an* + noun
Uncountable noun	**There is** some fantastic **food**. *There* **3** ________ *some* + noun	**There isn't** any **milk**. *There* **4** ________ *any* + noun
Plural noun	**There are** some great **food stands**. *There* **5** ________ *some* + noun	**There aren't** any **fries**. *There* **6** ________ *any* + noun

6 **Describe what you can see in the lunchbox.**

1 There ________ three tomatoes.
2 There ________ a sandwich.
3 There ________ any grapes.
4 There ________ some water.
5 There ________ a yogurt.
6 There ________ any rice.

7 **Complete the text with *there is/isn't* and *there are/aren't*. Use the words in bold to help you.**

My favorite lunch is a Bento box. **1** (...) different **menus** so **2** (...) any **problems** finding one you like. Apart from chicken and fish, **3** (...) a beef **bento box** and if you don't eat meat, **4** (...) a vegetarian **menu** too. **5** (...) **rice** in all the boxes: it's always included.

You can only buy the food to take home: **6** (...) a **restaurant**. And you must get there early. **7** (...) always a long **line** at lunchtime.

8 **Answer the question to solve the Brain teaser.**

BRAIN TEASER

2nd letter	3rd letter	2nd letter	4th letter	1st letter
l				

Look at the clues and write the correct letter. Then order the letters to make something you can eat.

What's the secret word?

Reinforcement and Challenge Grammar bootcamp p123

Places in a town

1 **Match the places in a town with the pictures.**

bike lane   bike station   bus stop
department store   fast-food restaurant
juice bar   library   museum   music venue
skate park   sports center   subway station

Cool places to live

What makes a city a great place to live? Schools, public transportation, places to eat – these all are important. The city review website has a list of places you can find in the best cities. Which of them do you have where you live?

2 **Where do you go ... ?**

1 to eat and drink
2 to exercise
3 to enjoy the arts

3 **Add one word to complete the places.**

1 bus/subway/train/gas/police/bike ________
2 town/shopping/sports/medical/city ________

4 **Work in pairs. Take turns describing a place. Can your partner guess what it is?**

This is a place to do aerobics.

I know, it's a sports center. My turn!

An informal conversation

Subskill: Predicting vocabulary

Before you listen, think about the words you expect to hear.

5 **Read the instructions in exercise 6. What words and phrases do you expect to hear in the conversation?**

6 33 **Mia is planning to visit her cousin Ethan in Buenos Aires. Listen and order the things that they talk about.**

a food
b music
c sports
d transportation

7 **Listen again. Complete the notes.**

- *sports center near Ethan – yes or no? 1* ________
- *How many? 2* ________
- *soccer – yes or no? 3* ________
- *street food near him – yes or no? 4* ________
- *the best way to get to the city center? 5* ________
- *live music near him? 6* ________
- *things to take? 7* ________ *and 8* ________

8 **Listen again and answer the questions.**

1 What other place for sports is there near Ethan?
2 Where can Mia and Ethan go to eat and meet friends?
3 What food does Ethan recommend?
4 What is the fastest way to go to the city center?
5 Is it dangerous to bike in the city? Why/Why not?
6 Where can Mia and Ethan hear live music?

9 **Work in pairs. What are the advantages and disadvantages of your town or city? Is it a good place to live? Think about:**

- places to play sports
- places to eat
- transportation
- places to go out

FUN FACTS

Buenos Aires has 130 km of bike lanes. That's perfect to explore the city by bike!

Is there ... ? Are there ... ?

1 **Complete the table with *is*, *are*, *isn't* or *aren't*.**

<table>
<tr><th colspan="3">Questions and short answers</th></tr>
<tr><td>Singular nouns</td><td>Is there a sports center?</td><td rowspan="2">Yes, there is./
No, there
2 ________ .</td></tr>
<tr><td>Uncountable nouns</td><td>1 ________ there any street food?</td></tr>
<tr><td rowspan="2">Plural nouns</td><td>3 ________ there five soccer teams?</td><td rowspan="2">Yes, there are./
No, there
4 ________ .</td></tr>
<tr><td>Are there any bike lanes?</td></tr>
</table>

2 **Complete the questions with *Is there* or *Are there*.**

1 ________ a 3D movie theater where you live?
2 ________ any skate parks?
3 ________ any museums?
4 ________ a lot of traffic in the city center?

3 **Write short answers to the questions in exercise 2 so they are true for you.**

4 **Write the questions for the answers using *a* or *any*. Then write short answers.**

1 There's a sports center near my home.
Is there a sports center near your home?
Yes, there is.
2 There isn't a subway in my town.
3 There are some fast-food restaurants.
4 There aren't any juice bars.
5 There isn't any good live music.

How much/many ... ?

5 **Read the sentences in the table and circle the correct option to complete the rules.**

Questions	Answers
How much traffic is there?	A lot/Some/Not much.
How many bike lanes are there?	A lot/Some/Not many.

1 We use *How much* with **countable/ uncountable** nouns.
2 We use *How many* with **countable/ uncountable** nouns.

6 **Complete the questions with *How much* or *How many*. Then answer the questions.**

1 ________ department stores are there in your town?
2 ________ public transportation is there?
3 ________ open space is there?
4 ________ libraries are there?
5 ________ skate parks are there?

7 **Write questions with *How much* and *How many*.**

1 brothers and sisters / you / have ?
2 homework / you / do / on weekends ?
3 time / you / spend / watching TV ?
4 comic books or magazines / you / read ?
5 fruit / you / eat / every day ?

8 **Work in pairs. Ask and answer the questions in exercise 7.**

9 **Circle the correct option.**

GRAMMAR ROUND-UP

1 2 3 4 5 6 7 8

The happiest city in the world!

Melbourne, Madrid and New York City are all fun places to live, but the **1** (...) place, according to a recent survey, is Chicago.

2 (...) a lot of places to eat, and the city is famous for its delicious street food. It **3** (...) cost a lot. In fact, Chicago is cheaper **4** (...) many other cities in the USA.

There are **5** (...) fun things to do on weekends. You can take a boat on the river or walk around Millennium Park. If you like **6** (...) , you can also see the park by bike. Or why not go to the top of the Willis Tower? You **7** (...) stand outside the building in a glass box. How many cities offer an experience like that?

1 a good b best c better
2 a It's b There's c There are
3 a don't b isn't c doesn't
4 a than b of c that
5 a a b some c any
6 a bike b go biking c biking
7 a can't b can c must

Asking for directions

1 **Look at the map of a town and write the places.**

1 It's **across from** the supermarket.
2 It's **next to** the juice bar.
3 It's **between** the police station and the hotel.
4 It's **on the corner** of West Avenue and Well Street.

2 **Watch the video and follow Archie's route on the map. Start from 'You are here'.**

3 **Watch again. Which Key phrases do you hear?**

4 **Complete the dialogue with the Key phrases. Watch again and check.**

Archie
Excuse me. Can you tell me how **1** ________________ the library?

Person 1
Let's see. Yes, go **2** ________________ , along Station Road. Turn left into Well Street. There's a museum on the corner, you can't miss it.

Archie
OK, along Station Road, then left.

Person 1
That's right. Go along Well Street, and **3** ________________ the skate park. Then **4** ________________ and it's there, near the sports centre.

Archie
Great, thanks.

Excuse me. **5** ________________ a library near here?

Person 2
Yes. Go along this road and turn right. It's **6** ________________ , opposite the police station.

Archie
Cheers!

5 **Create your own dialogue. Follow the steps in the Skills boost.**

SKILLS BOOST

THINK
You are outside the school on the map. Choose a place that you want to go to.

PREPARE
Prepare a dialogue.

PRACTICE
Practice the dialogue. Take turns giving directions.

PERFORM
Act out your dialogue for the class.

6 **Peer review** **Listen to your classmates and answer the questions.**

1 Follow on the map. Are the directions clear?
2 How many Key phrases do they use?

Key phrases

Asking for directions: Excuse me. Can you tell me how to get to the (library)?
Is there a (library) near here?

Giving directions: Go straight ahead.
Turn left/right.
Go past the (skate park).
It's on your left/right.

UK → US

sports centre (UK) → **sports center** (US)
Go along Well Street. (UK) → **Go down** Well Street. (US)
It's **opposite** the police station. (UK) → It's **across from** the police station. (US)

Voices

The Question: What is your favorite place to visit?

My favorite place to visit is Brighton. My cousins live there, and I usually stay with them for my vacation.

It's a small town on the south coast of England, but there are lots of things to do. There's a modern part with a department store and busy restaurants, and there's an old part. I prefer the old part because it's full of interesting shops and cafés. My favorite place sells ice cream – it has more than 20 different flavors.

Brighton also has a beach. It's quiet in the winter, but it can get crowded in the summer. I usually go there with my cousins in the summer and we play volleyball or swim in the ocean. There's an amusement park near the beach too.

I think Brighton is a beautiful and exciting place. I really recommend that you visit it!

Jayden, United States

A description of a place

1 **Work in pairs. What makes a good place to visit? Make a list of things you like.**

2 **Read Jayden's description of Brighton. Would you like to visit this place? Why/Why not?**

3 **Read the description again and complete the sentences.**

1 Jayden often visits Brighton because _________ .
2 He likes the old part because _________ .
3 He likes his favorite shop because _________ .
4 He usually goes to _________ with his cousins in the summer.
5 They like _________ there.
6 He thinks that Brighton is _________ .

▶ Subskill: Adjectives

Adjectives help to make a description more interesting. Adjectives come before a noun, e.g. *There are a lot of interesting stores.*

4 **Find ten adjectives to describe a place in the text.**

5 **Match the adjectives in exercise 4 with definitions 1–5.**

1 new, from the present time _________
2 with a lot of something _________
3 with more people than you want _________
4 without noise or people _________
5 with a lot of fun activities _________

6 **The words in bold are in the wrong sentence. Correct the sentences.**

1 The cafés are always **beautiful** at lunchtime. _________
2 There are **modern** flowers and trees in the park. _________
3 Some of the buildings are **small**, but most of them are old. _________
4 The department store isn't big. In fact, it's **exciting** for a town this size. _________
5 There aren't many cars or people so it's very **busy**. _________
6 It's never boring. It's always **quiet**! _________

7 **Write about your favorite place to visit. Follow the steps in the Skills boost.**

SKILLS BOOST

THINK

1 Think of your favorite place to visit. It can be a place where you go on vacation or that you visit on weekends.

2 Make notes. Answer the questions.

- Why do you go there?
- Is it big or small?
- What places are there?
- What do you usually do there?
- What can you eat and drink there?
- Why do you like it?

____

____

____

PREPARE

Organize your ideas into paragraphs.

Paragraph 1: The place/Why you go there

____

____

Paragraph 2: A general description/Your favorite places

____

____

Paragraph 3: Eating and drinking

____

____

Paragraph 4: Why you like it

____

____

WRITE

Write your description. Remember to use adjectives.

My favorite place to visit is … . I usually go there because …

CHECK

Read your description. Answer the questions.

1 Do you use vocabulary of places in a town? ☐

2 Do you use *there is/are* correctly? ☐

3 Do you use adjectives to describe the place? ☐

8 **Peer review** **Exchange your description with other students. Which place would you like to visit? Why?**

Quick review

Grammar

Countable and uncountable nouns

Countable nouns are nouns that we can count.
bananas, eggs, fries, peas
Uncountable nouns are nouns that we can't count.
butter, milk, pasta, sauce

a, an, some/any

With singular countable nouns, use *a* or *an*.
*Can I have **a banana**, please?*
With uncountable nouns, use *some/any* or *no article*.
*I usually have **some milk** for breakfast. (affirmative)*
*We don't have **any butter** in the fridge. (negative)*
*Is there **any cake**? (question)*
*We usually have **pasta** for dinner. (no article)*

there is/are

We use *there is* or *there isn't* before singular nouns and uncountable nouns.
***There's** a food stand near my home.*
***There isn't** any sauce on the pasta.*
We use *there are* or *there aren't* before plural nouns.
***There are** some great places to buy street food.*
***There aren't** any fries.*

Is there … ? Are there … ?

We use *Is there … ?* with singular and uncountable nouns.
***Is there** a skate park?* *Yes, **there is**./No, **there isn't**.*
***Is there** any street food?*
We use *Are there … ?* with plural nouns.
***Are there** any buses?* *Yes, **there are**./No, **there aren't**.*
We use *How much* to ask about quantity with uncountable nouns.
***How much** traffic is there?* *A lot/Some/Not **much**.*
We use *How many* to ask about numbers with countable nouns.
***How many** museums are there?* *A lot/Some/Not **many**.*

Vocabulary

34 Food and drink

banana, beef, butter, cake, cheese, chicken, chocolate, eggs, fries, grapes, herbs, ice cream, melon, milk, mushroom, noodles, oil, onion, pasta, peas, rice, sauce, spices, yogurt

35 Places in a town

bike lane, bike station, bus stop, department store, fast-food restaurant, juice bar, library, museum, music venue, skate park
bus/gas/police/subway/train station
city/medical/shopping/sports/town center

5 Project

WDYT?
(What do you think?)

What makes a town a good place to live in?

TASK: Make a map showing useful places for young people moving to live in your town.

Learning outcomes

1 I can give information about places in my town.
2 I can think about other people's needs.
3 I can use appropriate language from the unit.

Graphic organizer → Project planner p132

1 Watch a video of students presenting a map of their town. Would you like to live there? Why/Why not?

STEP 1: THINK

2 Look at the map in the Model project and add the places to the diagram.

3 Add any more places to the categories.

STEP 2: PLAN

4 Work in groups of three. Decide to create a map of:

a all of your town
b a part of your town

5 Work in groups. Read the tips in the Super skills box and practice saying the Key phrases with your group.

CRITICAL THINKING — SUPER SKILLS

Considering the needs of other people

Tips

Think about what other people like.
Include ideas for different people.
Think about what young people moving to your town need to know.

Key phrases

Don't forget ...
What about somewhere for people who ... ?
I think we need something for someone who ...
That's a good idea.
There aren't any places for ...
Let's add something about (transportation).

6 Make your own diagram of places to include (see exercise 2). Use the tips and Key phrases in the Super skills box.

STEP 3: CREATE

7 Make your map. Remember:

- You can copy from an online map if you want.
- Make the map clear and attractive.
- You can include pictures or photos of the places.
- Write information boxes with more information about the places on your map.

Grammar and Vocabulary Quick review p69

Model project

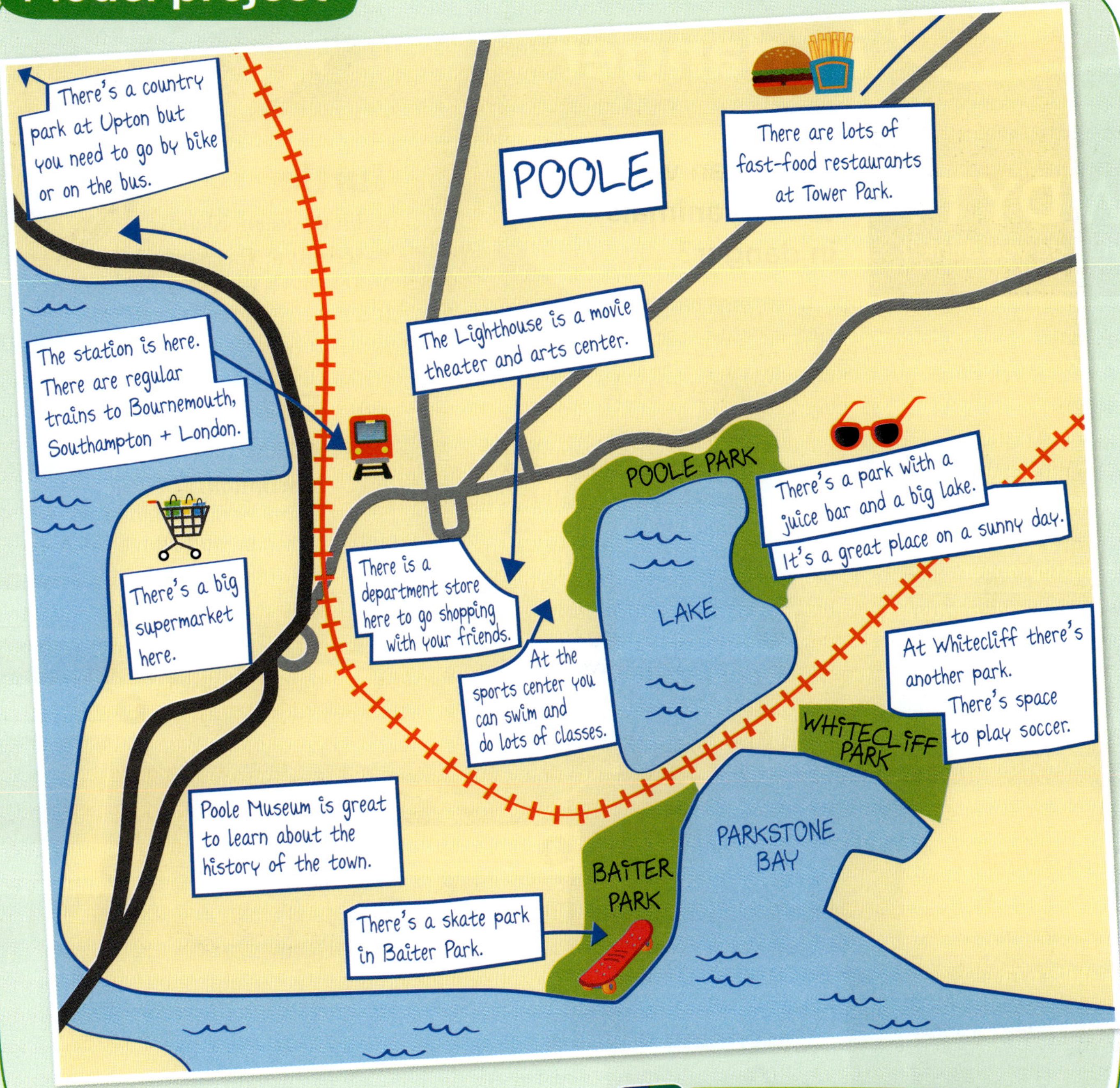

STEP 4: PRESENT

8 **Read the *How to ...* tips on p132. Then work with another group. Take turns to present your map.**

9 Peer review **As you listen to your classmates, answer the questions.**

1 Do you think the information is useful for young people moving to live in your town?

2 Ask a question about one of the places.

5 FINAL REFLECTION

1 The task

Is the map clear and attractive?

Do you give useful information about your town?

2 Super skill

Do you include ideas for different people? Give examples.

3 Language

Do you use language from the unit? Give examples.

6 Animals in danger

WDYT?
(What do you think?)

What can we do to help animals in danger?

Vocabulary: describing animals; collocations: taking action

Grammar: simple past of *be* and regular verbs

Reading: an article about two conservation success stories

Listening: a podcast about a teen entrepreneur

Speaking: showing interest

Writing: an email

Project: prepare a poster about endangered animals

Video skills p73

Real-world speaking p79

Project pp82–83

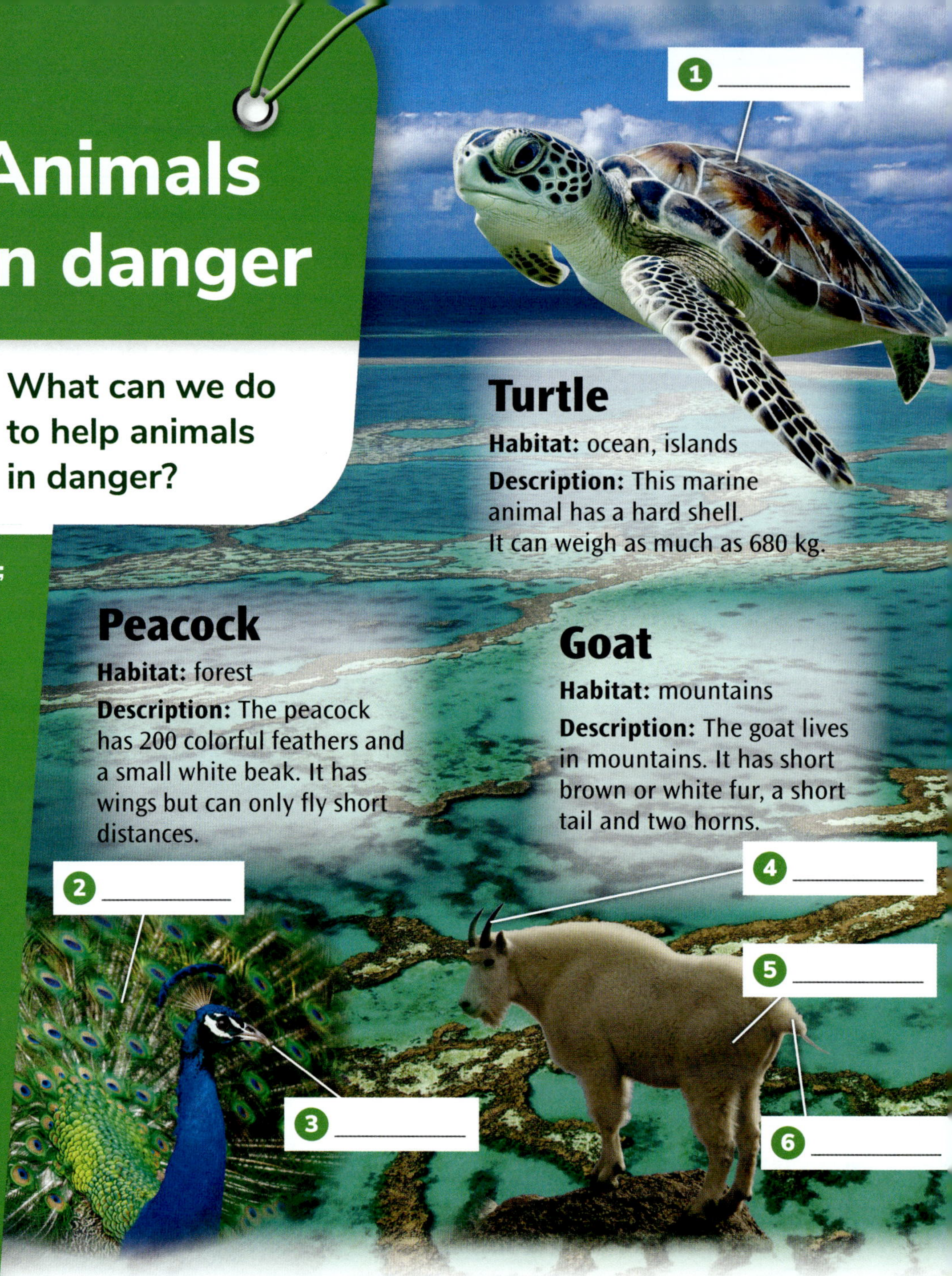

Turtle

Habitat: ocean, islands

Description: This marine animal has a hard shell. It can weigh as much as 680 kg.

Peacock

Habitat: forest

Description: The peacock has 200 colorful feathers and a small white beak. It has wings but can only fly short distances.

Goat

Habitat: mountains

Description: The goat lives in mountains. It has short brown or white fur, a short tail and two horns.

Describing animals

1 Read the mini texts and write the names of the animals in the table.

Class	Animal	Class	Animal
bird		insect	
mammal	*goat*	reptile	

2 Add the animals in the box to the table. Which animal can't you add? Why not?

ant crocodile parrot penguin rhinoceros shark

3 Read the descriptions and match the words in the box to body parts 1–9 in the photos.

beak feathers fin fur horn shell tail tooth/teeth wings

Bee

Habitat: garden, the countryside

Description: The bee has a yellow and black striped body. It makes honey and is very important for plants.

7 ________

8 ________

Dolphin

Habitat: ocean, rivers

Description: The dolphin lives in the ocean. It has a big fin on its back, but it's not a fish. It has up to 100 teeth. It's very intelligent.

9 ________

Snake

Habitat: deserts, forests

Description: Snakes are often dangerous. This spotted rattlesnake is very poisonous and can kill you.

4 **Match the adjectives we can use to describe animals with the correct symbol.**

colorful dangerous marine
poisonous spotted striped

1 
2 
3 
4 
5 
6 

be* and *have

We say 'The tiger *is* a striped animal' but 'It *has* striped fur.'

5 36 **Listen to the descriptions and write the name of each animal.**

6 **Complete the descriptions of animals using words from the box.**

beak colorful dangerous
feathers horns tail (x2) wings

The parrot is a very **1** ________ bird with yellow **2** ________ on its body. It has a black **3** ________ , blue **4** ________ and a long blue **5** ________ .

The rhino has two **6** ________ and a very short **7** ________ . It's a big animal and can be very **8** ________ if it gets angry.

7 **Work in pairs. Student A, think of an animal. Student B, ask questions to guess your partner's animal.**

Is it a mammal? — No, it isn't.
Is it a bird? — Yes, it is.
Is it colorful? — Yes, it is.
I know – it's a peacock! — Yes!

VIDEO SKILLS

8 **Watch the video. What animals do you see?**

9 **Work in pairs. Discuss the questions.**

1 Why do vloggers make top 5 videos?
2 Why are top 5 videos popular?
3 What could you make a top 5 video about?
4 Do you like this video? Why/Why not?

An article

1 Work in pairs. Answer the quiz questions.

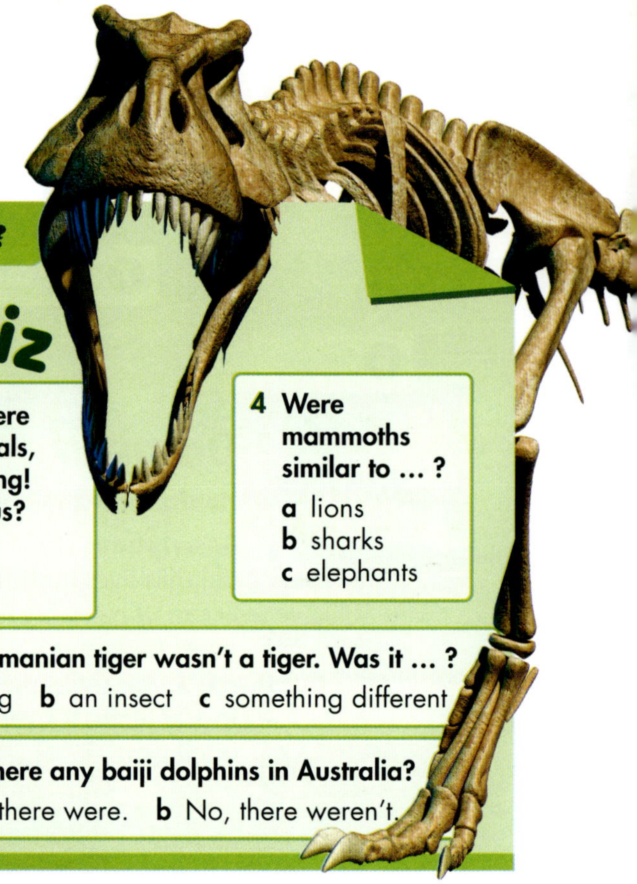

How much do you know about extinct animals?

Amazing animals of the past Quiz

1 Which dinosaur was the biggest?
- a the Titanosaur
- b the Tyrannosaurus Rex
- c the Stegosaurus

2 Was the dodo … ?
- a a reptile b a mammal c a bird

3 Steller's sea cows were very big sea mammals, up to nine meters long! Were they dangerous?
- a Yes, they were.
- b No, they weren't.

4 Were mammoths similar to … ?
- a lions
- b sharks
- c elephants

5 The Tasmanian tiger wasn't a tiger. Was it … ?
- a a dog b an insect c something different

6 Were there any baiji dolphins in Australia?
- a Yes, there were. b No, there weren't.

2 37 **Listen and check your answers.**

3 38 **Read and listen to the article about two animals. What do they have in common?**

▶ Subskill: Understanding the content of paragraphs

Read the headings first, then read paragraph A to see which fits best.

4 **Match headings 1–5 with paragraphs A–E in the article.**

1. Can we change this situation?
2. What are the facts about gorillas?
3. What solutions were there to the problems?
4. What is a saiga?
5. Why were saigas and gorillas in danger?

5 **Which animal does the information refer to? Write G (gorilla) or S (saiga).**

1. In the 1900s, the population was over a million. __
2. They sometimes travel 1,000 km. __
3. There were 500 in 1960. __
4. There were 50,000 in the year 2000. __
5. There were about 200 in the 1970s. __

6 **Are the sentences true or false? Correct the false sentences.**

1. The saiga has a very small nose.
2. The gorilla has gray fur.
3. The reasons for changes in saiga and gorilla populations were habitat and hunting.
4. The populations of both animals are improving.
5. The saiga and gorilla are the only success stories.

7 Word work **Match the definitions to the words in bold in the text.**

1. a program of activities ________
2. the number of people or animals living somewhere ________
3. killing an animal for food or sport ________
4. rules made by a government ________
5. the place where an animal lives ________
6. very hot, dry places ________

8 **Complete the sentences with words from exercise 7.**

1. The Sahara and the Gobi are ________ .
2. Oceans and rivers are the ________ of the dolphin.
3. I don't like ________ or killing animals.
4. I'm organizing a ________ to get people to bike to school.
5. We need more ________ to control the internet.
6. The ________ of my city is 700,000.

CRITICAL THINKING SUPER SKILLS

1. **Remember** Find examples in the article of actions to help animals in danger.
2. **Evaluate** Think of an advantage and a disadvantage of each action. Then choose the best idea.
3. **Create** Imagine you are creating a campaign to help animals in danger. Which animals would you help? Why?

The saiga and the mountain gorilla

Two conservation success stories

Some scientists say that one species becomes extinct every seven minutes.
What can we do to stop this from happening?
Let's meet two endangered animals and find out.

A ________

The saiga has brown or gray fur, horns and a very strange long nose. It lives in groups in the **deserts** of south-east Europe and central Asia. They can travel up to 1,000 km between summer and winter. In the 1990s there were more than a million saigas, but by the year 2000 the population was less than 50,000.

B ________

The mountain gorilla is a large mammal. It lives in national parks in two regions of Africa. It has black fur and is very intelligent. In 1960 there were about 500 gorillas in the Virunga mountains, but by the 1970s the **population** was about 200.

C ________

The saiga and the gorilla were both at risk of extinction. The reduction in **habitat** was a big problem: there wasn't enough open space for the saiga and there was less forest for the gorilla. **Hunting** was also a serious problem. Some people kill gorillas or sell them. There weren't any **laws** to stop this until 2008. Other people kill saigas for their horns.

FUN FACTS

Mountain gorillas can weigh 180 kg.

Gearing up 4 for Gorillas

Logo of G4G, a mountain gorilla charity organization

D ________

Animal conservation organizations, like WWF®, and governments were very worried and there was a big **campaign** to help the saiga and the gorilla, with more money to protect their habitats and new laws to stop hunting. There were special exhibits and there was even a saiga stamp!

E ________

The saiga and mountain gorilla are still in danger but the populations are slowly growing. And the saiga and the gorilla are not the only success stories: a similar program is also helping the giant panda. Extinction of plants and animals is still a very serious problem, but with success stories like these, we can see that change is possible.

Saiga postage stamp from Mongolia

Simple past: *be*

1 Complete the tables with the examples in the box.

Steller's sea cows **were** very big sea mammals.
The Tasmanian tiger **wasn't** a tiger.
There **was** less forest for the gorilla.
There **were** more than a million saigas.

Affirmative and negative		
Subject	**was(n't)**	**+ singular**
Hunting 1	was	a serious problem.
Subject	**were(n't)**	**+ plural**
2		

there was/were		
There	**was(n't)**	**+ singular**
3		
There	**were(n't)**	**+ plural**
There 4	weren't	any laws.

2 Complete the sentences with the correct simple past form of *be*.

1 The dodo ________ an unusual bird from Mauritius. It ________ one meter tall.
2 Mammoths ________ reptiles; they ________ mammals.
3 By 2002, there ________ any baiji dolphins. They ________ extinct.
4 Steller's sea cow ________ a cow. It ________ a big mammal and its habitat ________ the sea.

3 Read the examples. Circle the correct option to complete the rules.

Yes/No questions	Short answers
Were they dangerous?	No, they **weren't**.
Was the dodo a bird?	Yes, it **was**.
Were there any baiji dolphins in Australia?	No, there **weren't**.
Wh- questions	
What **was** the problem?	
How many saigas **were** there in 1990?	

1 In Yes/No questions, the verb comes **first/second**.
2 In Wh- questions, the verb comes **before/after** the question word (who, what, why, etc.).
3 When we ask questions with there was/were, the verb comes **before/after** there.

4 Order the words to make questions.

1 was / How / big / rhino / the ?
2 dangerous / Was / it ?
3 the / What / rhino's / diet / was ?
4 were / there / rhinos / in / 2011 / many / How ?
5 in Cameroon / there / Were / rhinos ?

5 Match answers a–e to questions 1–5 in exercise 4.

a Plants. __
b None. They were extinct. __
c It was up to 3.8 m long. __
d Yes, there were. __
e Yes, because it was so big. __

6 Complete the text with *was(n't)* or *were(n't)*.

Today on the Fun Facts Forum we answer your questions about

PREHISTORIC ANIMALS

Which **1** ________ the most frightening animal?
Keisha, Boston

I think it **2** ________ the megalodon, from the shark family. Megalodons **3** ________ very dangerous. Their name means 'big tooth'! It **4** ________ a good idea to go near them!

5 ________ dinosaurs the biggest reptiles?
Cameron, Glasgow

Yes, they **6** ________ . But they **7** ________ the most dangerous! There **8** ________ an enormous dinosaur-eating crocodile called Deinosuchus.

9 ________ the dodo the only flightless bird?
Laurie, Vancouver

No, it **10** ________ . There **11** ________ a prehistoric bird that was too big to fly! The Ornimegalonyx was more than 9 kg.

7 Answer the question to solve the Brain teaser.

BRAIN TEASER

All the mammoths were in a line. Two mammoths were in front of a mammoth. Two mammoths were behind a mammoth. And there was a mammoth in the middle.

What is the smallest possible number of mammoths?

Reinforcement and Challenge Grammar bootcamp p124

Collocations: taking action

1 **Complete the brochure with verbs in the box.**

donate join organize protect raise solve start visit

Save our wildlife!

There are many ways that we can **1** ________ wildlife. Why not choose two and do them in the next month?

How you can help

- Find out which animals are in danger and what you can do to **2** ________ the problem.
- **3** ________ a wildlife park and see animals in real life.
- **4** ________ an organization like the World Wildlife Fund® and help them with their work.
- **5** ________ a new school club. Meet regularly and talk about animals.
- **6** ________ a special day at your school with games and activities to teach other students about wildlife.
- **7** ________ money to give to a wildlife charity.
- **8** ________ a small amount of money every month and help to save your favorite animal.

2 **Match verbs 1–8 with nouns a–h to form collocations.**

1 visit	**a** a group, a club
2 join	**b** endangered animals, birds
3 organize	**c** awareness, money
4 protect	**d** old clothes, your time
5 start	**e** a zoo, a museum
6 donate	**f** a party, a sports event
7 raise	**g** a mystery, a puzzle
8 solve	**h** a new business, a blog

CELEBRITY CORNER

Soccer player **Raúl Jiménez** works to help Mexican wolves, an endangered species. Find out about another famous person who helps animals in danger.

A podcast

Subskill: Identifying which statements are true or false

Before you listen, read the true/false options and underline key words. As you listen, check the statements that are completely true. The remaining option must be the false one.

3 39 **Listen to a podcast about Mikaila Ulmer. Which two statements are true?**

a She's a young entrepreneur.
b She donates money to protect bees.
c She is a volunteer for a wildlife organization.

4 **Listen again. Are the sentences true or false? Correct the false sentences.**

1 You can only buy Mikaila's lemonade in Texas.
2 Bees were her favorite insect when she was young.
3 She decided to make lemonade for a business competition.
4 She used a recipe from her aunt's cookbook.
5 Cafés and shops now sell the drink.
6 The President of the USA tried her lemonade.

5 **Circle the correct option.**

1 Mikaila was **four/five** years old when it started.
2 She received $ **50,000/60,000** for her business on a TV show.
3 Mikaila has a contract for $ **7/11** million to sell her lemonade.
4 She gives **20/25** % of her money to bee organizations.
5 She visited the White House in **2016/2017**.

6 **Discuss the questions in pairs.**

1 In what ways is Mikaila extraordinary?
2 What's the most important thing she does?

Simple past of regular verbs: affirmative and negative

1 Read the examples and complete the rules.

Affirmative	Negative
She **started** to sell the drink.	She **didn't like** bees.
She **visited** the White House.	She **didn't stop** there.

1 For the simple past of regular verbs, add ______________ .

2 For the negative, use ______________ + base form.

2 Read the Spelling rules on p81. Write the affirmative simple past of the verbs in the box.

finish like organize play
study travel visit watch

3 Complete the sentences with the affirmative or negative of the verbs in parentheses.

1 I started my science project last weekend, but I ______________ **(finish)** it.

2 We ______________ **(watch)** a movie about pandas yesterday.

3 We ______________ **(play)** football last weekend because the weather was so bad.

4 My grandparents are on vacation now so we ______________ **(visit)** them last Sunday.

5 I ______________ **(like)** animals when I was younger but now I love them.

6 We ______________ **(organize)** an event at our school last term to raise money for wildlife.

Time expressions

We use the simple past with past time expressions.

yesterday, last night, last Thursday, last weekend, in August, in 2017

4 Write true sentences for you. Compare your sentences with other students.

1 watch TV / last night

2 play a computer game / last weekend

3 visit another country / last year

4 study English / last summer

5 listen to music / yesterday

6 travel by bus / last week

Irregular simple past verbs

Some verbs are irregular in the affirmative of the simple past.

go → went see → saw have → had meet → met

5 Circle the correct option.

GRAMMAR ROUND-UP

1 2 3 4 5 6 7 8

From zoos, to wildlife parks, to city farms, there **1 is/are/were** many places for animal-lovers to visit in the UK.

One of **2 more/the most/the best** exciting places is 'Crocodiles of the World', near Oxford. Here, you can see 150 crocodiles and other reptiles. **3 It was/There was/There were** the idea of Shaun Foggett, or 'The Croc Man'. Shaun had a collection of crocodiles at his home, but there **4 was/wasn't/weren't** space for all of them. He didn't **5 want/wants/wanted** to give the crocodiles to other people so he **6 decide/decides/decided** to start a zoo.

Now, Shaun **7 help/helps/helped** to protect the crocodiles and teach other people about them. Visitors can help take care of the animals – prepare their food and feed them. (You **8 can't/must not/must** be careful, of course!) You can also donate money to the organization.

Research

Where can you go to see animals in your local area?

Showing interest

1 Watch the video and circle the correct option.

1 Megan visited a **city farm/wildlife park/zoo**.

2 Lukas **went out with friends/studied/ played computer games**.

2 Watch again. Which Key phrases do you hear?

3 Complete the dialogue with the Key phrases. Watch again and check.

Lukas Hi, Megan. How was your weekend?

Megan Hi! It was brilliant! I went to a farm, right here in the city.

Lukas No **1** ________ ! What was **2** ________ ?

Megan It was cool! There were loads of animals. Look, I've got some photos.

Lukas Aww, that's **3** ________! **4** ________ funny!

Megan And this is me feeding the chickens. I wasn't very good at it. They nearly escaped!

Lukas You're **5** ________ !

Megan No, it's true! So, what about you?

Lukas Oh, I was at home the whole time.

Megan **6** ________ boring!

Lukas I know, but I finished my science project.

Megan Oh, no! Is that for today?

4 40 Listen and repeat the Key phrases. Pay attention to the intonation.

5 Create your own dialogue. Follow the steps in the Skills boost.

SKILLS BOOST

THINK
Choose a place in a city or the countryside that you visited. Make notes about it.

PREPARE
Prepare a dialogue. Include Key phrases for showing interest.

PRACTICE
Practice your dialogue. Remember to use intonation to show interest.

PERFORM
Act out your dialogue for the class.

6 Peer review Listen to your classmates and answer the questions.

1 Which Key phrases do they use?

2 Do they use intonation to show interest?

Key phrases

Asking questions: What was it like?
Was it fun?
Responding: You're (kidding/joking)!
Really? No way!
That's so funny!
That's (amazing/cute/great)!
Sounds (boring/interesting/incredible)!

UK → US

It was **brilliant**. (UK) → It was **awesome**. (US)
There were **loads** of animals. (UK) → There were **lots** of animals. (US)

Josef To: Sam Friday Attachments 1.4MB

Hi Sam,

How are things? We went on a school trip to the National Aquarium last week. It was awesome! There were lots of fish. The sharks were definitely the best!

First of all, we visited the local fish section and learned about their habitats. Then we saw the jellyfish. They were really cool, especially the white-spotted jellyfish. After that, we went to the Atlantic Ocean tank. It's the biggest tank in the country and we actually walked under the water. There were sharks and stingrays above our heads. It was amazing!

Next, there were the smaller tanks with colorful tropical fish and a giant octopus. Finally, we saw the turtles before we went home. I'm sending you a picture of one of them. I hope you like it!

Anyway, that's all for now. Let me know your news.

Talk later,

Josef

An email

1 Read the email about a school trip to an aquarium and answer the questions.

1 What marine animals does Josef mention?

2 What adjectives does he use to give his opinion?

2 Answer the questions.

1 When was Josef's trip?

2 What was his favorite marine animal?

3 What fish were there in the first section?

4 Which jellyfish was especially cool?

5 What two things were special about the Atlantic Ocean tank?

6 Were there tropical fish in the last tank?

3 Order the places that Josef visited.

a the jellyfish

b the turtles

c the section with local fish

d the smaller tanks

e the Atlantic Ocean tank

▶ Subskill: Sequencing words

We use sequencing words to describe the order of events, e.g. *First, ...*

4 Find five sequencing words in Josef's email.

5 Read the plan for a visit to a theme park. Write sentences using sequencing words and the simple past.

Last week, we went to a theme park. It was awesome! First, ...

Theme park visit

10:30	Visit the 'Lost Kingdom' section and see 'living' dinosaurs
11:00	Go on the two giant rollercoasters there
1:00	Have lunch in the picnic area
1:45	Walk to the water attractions and go on the water slides
3:30	Meet in the animal arena and watch the keepers feed the penguins

6 **Write an email about a trip. Follow the steps in the Skills boost.**

SKILLS BOOST

THINK

1 Choose a place that you visited.

2 Make notes about where you went and the things you saw.

____

____

____

PREPARE

Organize your notes into paragraphs:

Paragraph 1: Where? / When? / Your favorite thing

____

____

____

____

____

____

____

Paragraph 2 and 3: The places you went to and the things you saw

____

____

____

____

____

____

____

____

WRITE

Write your email. Use the example in exercise 1 to help you.

Hi …

How are things? I/We went on a trip to …

CHECK

Read your email. Answer the questions.

1 Do you use *was/were* correctly? ☐

2 Do you use the simple past ending of regular verbs? ☐

3 Do you use irregular verbs in the past? ☐

4 Do you use sequencing words, e.g. *First of all, … , Then … ?* ☐

7 **Peer review** **Exchange your email with another student. Would you like to visit this place? Why/Why not?**

Quick review

Grammar

Simple past: *be*

I/He/She/It was/wasn't …

*The Titanosaur **was** the biggest dinosaur.*

You/We/They were/weren't …

*Mammoths **weren't** elephants.*

(Question word) + *was/were* + subject

***Were** mammoths big?* *Yes, they **were**./No, they **weren't**.*

*How big **were** they?*

there was/were

There was/wasn't + singular/uncountable noun

***There was** a problem.*

There were/weren't + plural noun

***There were** only 50,000 saigas.*

Was there + singular noun ?	*Yes, there was.* *No, there wasn't.*
***Was there** a big population?*	*No, **there wasn't.***
Were there + plural noun ?	*Yes, there were.* *No, there weren't.*
***Were there** saigas in Europe?*	*Yes, **there were.***

Simple past: regular verbs

Affirmative: verb + *-ed*

*She **started** a business.*

Negative: *didn't* (did not) + base form

*They **didn't visit** a wildlife park.*

Spelling rules

For most regular verbs, add *-ed* *visit → **visited***

Verbs ending in *-e* → + *-d* *receive → **received***

Verbs ending in a consonant + *-y* → y + *-ied*

*carry → **carried***

Some verbs ending in consonant + vowel + consonant → double the final consonant + *-ed*

*stop → **stopped*** *plan → **planned***

Vocabulary

41 Animals

Birds: parrot, peacock, penguin
Mammals: dolphin, goat, rhinoceros
Reptiles: crocodile, snake, turtle
Fish: shark
Insects: ant, bee

42 Describing animals

Body parts: beak, feathers, fin, fur, horn, shell, tail, tooth/teeth, wings
Adjectives: colorful, dangerous, marine, poisonous, spotted, striped

43 Collocations: taking action

donate money/old clothes/your time
join a club/a group/an organization
organize a party/special day/sports event
protect birds/endangered animals/wildlife
raise awareness/money
solve a mystery/problem/puzzle
start a blog/business/school club
visit a museum/wildlife park/zoo

6 Project

WDYT?
(What do you think?)

What can we do to help animals in danger?

TASK: Prepare a poster about endangered animals to raise awareness and help to protect them.

Learning outcomes

1 I can present clear information about endangered animals.

2 I can listen to my classmates' opinions.

3 I can use appropriate language from the unit.

Graphic organizer → Project planner p132

1 Watch a video of a student presenting a poster about endangered animals. Which animal(s) is it about?

STEP 1: THINK

2 Read the poster in the Model project. Which information does it include?

- a description of the animal
- its habitat
- its population (past and present)
- why it is in danger
- how the animal helps humans
- ways to help

3 Which of these things does the poster in the Model project include to make it interesting and attractive?

- title(s)
- pictures or photos
- maps
- diagrams
- text in short paragraphs
- numbers and statistics
- different fonts and colors

STEP 2: PLAN

4 Work in pairs and choose a class of animal to research.

5 Work individually. Research two endangered animals and make notes. Include the information in exercise 2.

STEP 3: CREATE

6 Work in pairs. Read the tips in the Super skills box and practice saying the Key phrases with a partner.

COLLABORATION — SUPER SKILLS

Listening to other people's opinions

Tips

Listen to others and ask questions.

Make decisions together.

Key phrases

That's a good idea.

Yes, that sounds good!

What do you think, (Miguel)?

Why do you think (this animal) is important?

Why don't we choose (the dolphin)?

Do we all agree?

So we've decided that …

7 Work in your pair. Share your research and choose two animals. Use the tips and Key phrases in the Super skills box.

8 Create your poster and prepare to talk about it.

Grammar and Vocabulary Quick review p81

Model project

Red pandas

Red pandas live in the forests of China, India, Nepal and Myanmar. They have red fur with black legs and a white striped face.

Red pandas are in danger because their natural habitat is disappearing, and with it, bamboo, their main food.

Fifty years ago, there were about 20,000 red pandas in the world, but now there are less than 10,000 (and some scientists say only 2,500).

To help to save them, you can join a wildlife organization and adopt a red panda, or campaign to stop the destruction of forests in Asia.

Sea otters

Sea otters are the smallest marine mammal, but they have very strong tails to help them swim. They live in the seas around Japan, Alaska, California and Mexico.

In the 1700s, there were between 150,000 and 300,000 of these otters, but people hunted them for their fur. In 1911, they were almost extinct.

The number of otters is growing again (there are about 100,000), but plastic in the oceans is now a problem. We need to teach people about plastic, and help to clean our beaches.

STEP 4: PRESENT

9 **Read the *How to ...* tips on p132. Then present your poster to the class.**

10 Peer review **Listen to the presentations of your classmates and answer the questions.**

1 Which animal do you like best? Why?
2 Think of a question to ask about the animals.

6 FINAL REFLECTION

1 The task

How attractive is your poster?

How easy is it to understand the presentation?

2 Super skill

How well do you collaborate? Give examples.

3 Language

Do you use language from the unit? Give examples.

7 Heroes

WDYT?
(What do you think?)

What makes a hero?

Vocabulary: jobs; adjectives to describe people

Grammar: simple past of irregular verbs; question forms and *ago*

Reading: a newspaper article about teen heroes

Listening: a podcast about two talented teens

Speaking: giving opinions

Writing: a biography

Project: make a presentation about a hero from the past

Video skills p85

Real-world speaking p91

Project pp94–95

BATMAN

Name: Bruce Wayne
Day job: 1 ________
Job description: He's very rich and has his own company.

CAPTAIN MARVEL

Name: Carol Danvers
Day job: 2 ________
Job description: She flies an airplane.

SUPERMAN

Name: Clark Kent
Day job: 3 ________
Job description: He writes newspaper articles for the *Daily Planet*.

Jobs

1 **Who am I? For each sentence, write the correct job in the box. There are three extra jobs.**

actor artist dentist doctor police officer receptionist singer taxi driver teacher waiter

1 I work in a school. I have classes with students. ________
2 I drive a car. I take people to different places. ________
3 I paint and draw and make pictures. ________
4 I work in a restaurant. I bring food to customers. ________
5 I take care of people's teeth. ________
6 I protect people and investigate crimes. ________
7 I greet people when they arrive at a hotel or office. ________

2 **Write sentences for the three extra jobs.**

____

____

____

SHURI

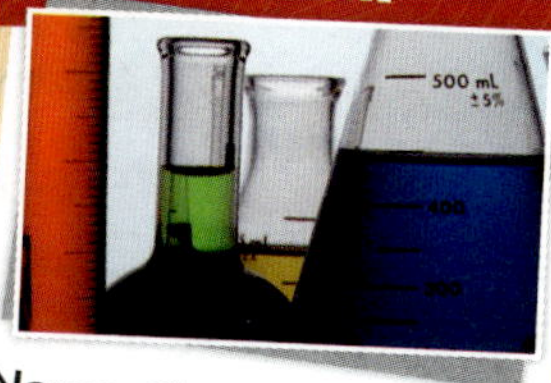

Name: Shuri
Day job: 4 ________
Job description: She invents things in her laboratory.

SPIDER-MAN

Name: Peter Parker
Day job: 5 ________
Job description: He takes photos for a newspaper.

IRON MAN

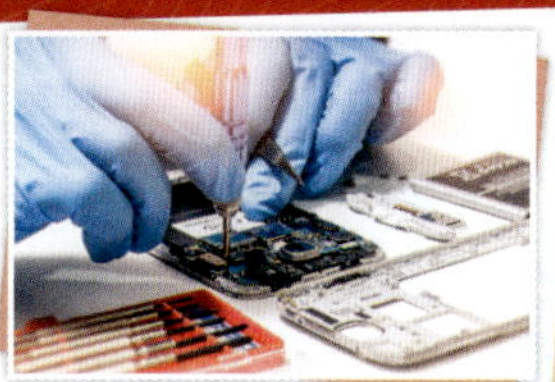

Name: Tony Stark
Day job: 6 ________
Job description: He designs new technology.

3 44 **Complete the day jobs of the six superheroes. Listen and check.**

businessman engineer journalist
photographer pilot scientist

4 Match 1–8 with a–h to make sentences.

1 A salesperson	a repairs cars and machines.
2 A chef	b takes care of sick people.
3 A web designer	c sells things in a store.
4 A manager	d organizes other workers.
5 A mechanic	e cooks in a restaurant.
6 An accountant	f works with money.
7 A nurse	g makes websites.
8 A lawyer	h helps people with legal problems.

5 Write jobs for each category.

1 **Five** people who wear a uniform or special clothes. *police officer, ...*
2 **Four** people who work in an office.
3 **Three** people who help people with their health.
4 **Two** people who work in a restaurant.
5 **One** person who works with machines.

6 Work in pairs. Ask *yes/no* questions to guess the job.

Do you work in an office?
No, I don't.
Do you work in a restaurant?
Yes, I do.
Do you cook food?
No, I don't.
Are you a waiter?
Yes, I am!

VIDEO SKILLS

7 Watch the video. What's the woman's job?

8 Work in pairs. Discuss the questions.

1 What kind of video is this?
   a a mini-documentary   b a vlog
   c an ad for a car
2 Which adjectives would you use to describe the video: interesting, boring, exciting, funny?
3 Who do you think would like this video?
4 How does the video make the woman interesting? Think about: how long you see each image, the sound effects, the voiceover, etc.

Pronunciation: Schwa /ə/ p129

A newspaper article

1 **Work in pairs. Answer the questions.**

1 What jobs help other people? (doctor, police officer ...)

2 Which three jobs do you think help people most? Why?

2 **Look at the photos on p87 and answer the questions.**

1 What was the weather like?

2 What problems do you think people had?

3 What jobs are important in these situations?

3 **Read the article quickly and circle the best headline.**

A **Police officers help people after storm**

B **TEEN HEROES RESCUE NEIGHBORS**

C **The people of Texas – the real heroes!**

4 45 **Read and listen to the article and answer the questions.**

1 Where was the storm?

2 What problems did people have after the storm?

3 Who were the teenage heroes?

4 How did they rescue people?

5 How many people did they rescue?

6 Did they only rescue people?

5 **Read the text again. Complete the sentences.**

1 When Thomas woke up, he saw that houses ______________________.

2 He used his boat because ______________.

3 Thomas and his friends went to houses when they heard ______________.

4 At first, the boys rescued people ______________.

5 After several hours, they also worked with ______________________.

6 People called the boys heroes after a photographer ______________.

▶ Subskill: Understanding new words

You can sometimes guess the meaning of new words in a text. Think about the general meaning of the sentence. Look at the words that come before and after the new word. Think about what type of word it is (adjective, verb, noun).

6 Word work **Find the words in bold in the text. What type of words are they? Can you guess their meaning?**

7 **Match the definitions to the words in bold.**

1 an adjective to describe a place or situation that is not dangerous ________

2 people who live in a town or city ________

3 an adjective to describe a person who does something in a dangerous situation ________

4 organizations that help people in dangerous situations ________

5 people who live near you ________

6 energy that makes light or machines work ________

8 **Complete the sentences with words from exercise 6.**

1 We can't use the computers today because there's no ________ .

2 I'm not afraid to go out at night. I live in a ________ place.

3 You must be ________ to go to a new country alone.

4 We saw one of our ________ at the concert.

5 The ________ of Texas are called Texans.

6 There are ________ to help people who get lost in the mountains.

CRITICAL THINKING SUPER SKILLS

1 **Understand** In what ways were the boys heroes? Find examples in the text.

2 **Apply** Do you think we can all be heroes in our daily lives? How can we do this? Think about:

school	free-time activities	vacations

3 **Evaluate** Can you think of other examples of ordinary heroes? Why are they heroes?

CELEBRITY CORNER

Beyoncé raised money with her charity BeyGOOD to help the victims of Hurricane Harvey. Find out about another celebrity who helped victims of a natural disaster.

THE DAILY WIRE

Houston, Texas • April 25th

When Hurricane Harvey came to Texas, it destroyed houses and roads. About 30,000 people left their homes before the storm, but others stayed. They didn't have drinking water or **electricity**, and they couldn't go outside because the streets were like rivers! In those difficult times, the **brave** Texan people helped each other, and many ordinary **citizens** became local heroes.

Among them were four teenage boys: 17-year-old Thomas Edwards and his friends, Richard, 17, Liam, 17 and his brother Declan, 15.

THE BOYS SPENT HOURS RESCUING THEIR NEIGHBORS.

The houses and streets of Texas under water after Hurricane Harvey

Thomas told journalists that he woke up that morning and saw houses under water. His car was under water too, but luckily, he had a small fishing boat. He called his friends and they decided to go out in the boat.

They began to look for people and take them to a **safe** place. Sometimes they heard calls for help. Other times, **neighbors** gave them addresses, or directions to the homes of family and friends.

For several hours, the boys worked alone, going from house to house. Later, they helped police officers and **rescue services**. In total, they saved at least 50 people, and even more pets. 'We rescued families, babies, dogs, rabbits,' said Thomas.

A photographer for a local newspaper saw the boys, and he posted photos of them on social media. People wrote comments, calling them heroes. Later, the boys said they didn't do it because they wanted to be heroes. They just wanted to help.

FOR US, THEY ARE TRUE LOCAL HEROES!

Simple past of irregular verbs: affirmative and negative

1 **Read the examples. Which of the verbs in blue are irregular?**

Thomas **woke up** that morning and **saw** houses under water.

He **had** a small boat.

They **decided** to go out in the boat.

2 **Complete the table with the affirmative or negative simple past form of the verbs in blue.**

Affirmative	Negative
People **left** their homes.	Others **didn't leave**.
Thomas **1** _______ early.	He **didn't wake up** late.
He **had** a small boat.	They **2** _______ electricity.
He **3** _______ houses under water.	He **didn't see** the streets.

3 **Write the affirmative simple past form of the irregular verbs in the box. Check your answers on pp134–135.**

begin come give ring
see spend take wake up

4 **Complete the sentences with some of the verbs in exercise 3.**

1 There was a storm and I ________ to feel afraid.
2 We ________ people on the roofs of houses.
3 I ________ my friend's doorbell.
4 He ________ to our house and ________ us to a safe place.

5 **Rewrite the underlined verbs from affirmative to negative and negative to affirmative.**

Pilot rescues hikers on mountain

Two women **1** <u>didn't meet</u> a real-life hero when they **2** <u>didn't go</u> on a hike one day to Table Mountain in the USA. One of the women **3** <u>didn't become</u> sick, and her friend **4** <u>knew</u> what to do, so she called for help. Luckily, a helicopter pilot **5** <u>didn't hear</u> the call. The helicopter arrived and **6** <u>didn't take</u> the sick woman to a safe place. The pilot was Harrison Ford!

6 **Write sentences in the affirmative or negative simple past so they are true for you.**

1 I / meet / friends last Saturday
I didn't meet friends last Saturday. I went to a museum with my brother.
2 I / see / a movie on TV last weekend
3 I / wake up / before nine o'clock on Sunday
4 We / have / pizza for dinner last week
5 I / spend / two hours doing homework last night

7 **Work in pairs. Compare your sentences in exercise 6. How many are the same?**

8 **Complete the article with regular and irregular verbs.**

Celebrity heroes

For me, Emma Watson is a hero in movies and in real life. After the Harry Potter movies **1** ________ **(come)** to an end, she **2** ________ **(be)** a millionaire. She **3** ________ **(decide)** she **4** ________ **(not want)** to just stay at home, so she **5** ________ **(go)** to college and **6** ________ **(study)** literature. Then she **7** ________ **(spend)** time in Zambia and Bangladesh promoting education for girls. She **8** ________ **(become)** a Goodwill Ambassador for the United Nations. She also **9** ________ **(give)** a million dollars to charity. Her career **10** ________ **(not stop)** after Harry Potter.

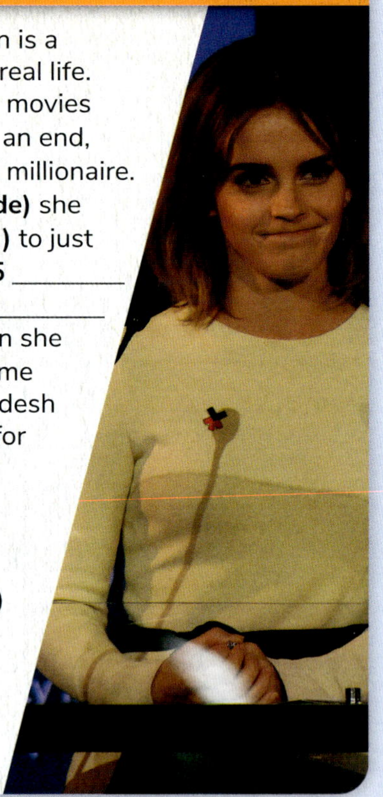

9 **Answer the question to solve the Brain teaser.**

BRAIN TEASER

A father and two children wanted to cross a river in a boat. The father weighed 90 kilos and each child weighed 45 kilos. The boat could only carry 90 kilos.

How did they cross the river?

Adjectives to describe people

1 **Read the dictionary definitions. Choose the correct adjective to describe people A–C.**

__ **generous** (adj.) giving people more of your time or money than is usual

__ **lazy** (adj.) not wanting to work

__ **talented** (adj.) very good at something

2 **Match the adjectives in the box with the definitions. Are the adjectives positive or negative?**

careful   friendly   kind   polite   special

1 You're not rude; you say "please" and "thank you". ______________

2 You're different, usually better, than what is normal. ______________

3 You think about what you are doing and try to avoid problems. ______________

4 You like to be with other people and make them feel happy. ______________

5 You think about other people and you always try to help them. ______________

3 **Match the words in the box with the adjectives in exercise 2 to make opposites.**

careless   normal   rude   unfriendly   unkind

4 **Write an adjective to describe each person.**

1 Helen's good at all kinds of sports, especially tennis. ________

2 My grandpa never drives fast and he respects other drivers. ________

3 Lara gives her money and her time to help others. ________

4 Ben never plays with his younger sister and he gets very impatient with her. ________

5 My brother never helps with the housework. ________

6 Alex often makes spelling mistakes because he doesn't check his homework. ________

A podcast

5 **Work in pairs. Look at the photos and describe what you can see.**

6 46 **Listen to the podcast. Complete each sentence with E (Easton) or A (Amineh).**

1 __ is from Colorado.

2 __ is from Syria.

3 __ moved to a different country.

4 __ tried to help someone.

5 __ started a business.

6 __ won a competition.

Subskill: Listening for numbers

Say the numbers in your head before you listen. You'll notice them better when listening.

7 **Listen again. Match each number with the correct information. There are two explanations you do not need.**

14   16   7 $80,000 $600   13   £1,000   1 year ago

1 normal cost of a robot hand

2 Easton's age when he met Momo

3 Amineh's age

4 number of robot hands Easton makes in a year

5 when Amineh started speaking English

6 number of people in Amineh's family

7 cost of Easton's hand

8 age when Easton made his first robot hand

9 prize in the poetry competition

10 Momo's age

8 **Discuss in pairs.**

1 Which person is more impressive?

2 Can we describe Easton and Amineh as heroes? Why/Why not?

Simple past: question forms and *ago*

1 **Complete the tables with the words in the box.**

question word verb *Did* *Yes/No* *did*

***Yes/No* questions and short answers**		
1 ________	**subject**	**2 ________ ?**
Did	it	**cost** a lot?
Did	she	**speak** English?
3 ________	**subject**	***did/didn't***
Yes,	it	**did**.
No,	she	**didn't**.

***Wh-* questions**			
4 ________	**5 ________**	**subject**	**verb**
When	**did**	they	**move**?

2 **Order the words to make questions.**

1 Easton / What / design / did ?
2 Amineh / a poem / Did / write ?
3 feel / How / Easton / did ?
4 cost / Momo's hand / did / How much ?
5 Amineh / speak / Did / in Syria / English ?

3 **Rewrite the sentences as questions with the words in bold.**

1 I got up at 7:30 am. **What time ...**
2 I watched TV at breakfast. **Did ...**
3 I went to school by bus. **How ...**
4 I had spaghetti for lunch. **What ...**
5 I saw my friends after school. **Who ...**

4 **Work in pairs. Ask your partner about what they did yesterday using the questions in exercise 3.**

5 **Order the time words in the box from shortest to longest.**

day hour minute month
second week year

ago

We use *ago* to say when we did something in the past. We can use different time words:
When did you start this class?
Ten minutes ago. An hour ago.

6 **Work in pairs. Combine words or phrases from each circle to make questions. Then ask your partner.**

1
When did you

2
start have
wake up
go

3
at this school
this class breakfast
on your last vacation
dinner last night
today

7 **Circle the correct option.**

GRAMMAR ROUND-UP

1 2 3 4 5 6 7 **8**

Yash Gupta **1** (...) in Los Angeles. He started wearing glasses when he **2** (...) five years old and he **3** (...) see well without them. When he was in high school, Yash broke his glasses in his taekwondo class and he didn't have **4** (...) glasses for a week. Yash realized how important his glasses were. He started thinking about people in other countries and he **5** (...) online that more than 12 million children do not have the glasses they need. When Yash **6** (...) 14, he started an organization called Sight Learning. The organization collects old glasses and sends **7** (...) to children in **8** (...) countries. Today more than 48,000 children can see better thanks to Sight Learning's glasses.

	a	b	c
1	living	live	lives
2	was	were	is
3	can't to	can't	doesn't can
4	some	any	many
5	reads	read	reading
6	was	ago	were
7	it	them	they
8	more poor	poorest	poorer

Research

Is there somewhere people can donate glasses where you live?

Giving opinions

1 Look at the photos and think of words you associate with this sport (people, verbs and things).

2 Watch the video. Do they like the same players?

3 Watch again. Which Key phrase is not in the dialogue?

4 Complete the dialogue with the Key phrases. Watch again and check.

Carmel
Did you see the football last night?

Louis
Yes, with the best player in the world. Mo Salah!

Carmel
Salah! There are lots of other good players. **1** ______________ Firmino?

Louis
OK. You've got a point – Firmino's pretty good. Who else?

Carmel
Mbappé for example, he played well yesterday. **2** ______________ there are lots of good French players.

Louis
Yes, I think you're **3** ______________ .

Carmel
And what do you think of Kanté? **4** ______________ , Kanté is better than Salah.

Louis
OK – Kanté is good, the French team is good, and Firmino's good. But there's still only one great player. The superstar. The best in the world. The Egyptian King – Salaaaaaah!

Carmel
5 ______________

5 Create your own dialogue. Follow the steps in the Skills boost.

SKILLS BOOST

THINK
Think about your favorite singers or athletes. Make notes about them.

PREPARE
Prepare a dialogue. Remember to include phrases for asking about and expressing opinions.

PRACTICE
Practice your dialogue.

PERFORM
Act out your dialogue for the class.

6 **Peer review** Listen to your classmates and answer the questions.

1 Who do they talk about?
2 Which Key phrases do they use to express opinions?
3 Do you agree with their opinions?

Key phrases

Asking for opinions: What do you think of ... ?
What about ... ?
Giving opinions: I (don't) think ...
If you ask me, ...
Agreeing: Yes, I think you're right about that.
You've got a point.
Disagreeing: No way!
That's ridiculous.

UK → US

Did you see the **football** last night? (UK) → Did you see the **soccer game** last night? (US)

Gertrude (Trudy) Ederle was born in New York in 1905. Her parents were from Germany and she was one of six children.

Trudy loved swimming and at the age of 12, she started training at the Women's Swimming Association. Swimming was not a popular women's sport at the time, but Trudy was a very talented swimmer. She broke eight world records and won an Olympic gold medal.

When she was 19, Trudy Ederle became the first woman to swim the English Channel. Normally, this is a very difficult 34 km swim. The day Trudy swam, the weather was terrible and she swam a total distance of 56 km! It took her 14 hours and 34 minutes. Trudy was the first woman and her time was also two hours quicker than the men's record.

After her swim, Trudy was a hero in the United States, but her later life was quiet. She taught swimming to deaf children for many years and died in 2003.

A biography

1 Read the biography and circle the best title.

- a The longest swim
- b A sports hero
- c Trudy loved swimming

2 Answer the questions.

1. Where was Trudy born?
2. How many brothers and sisters did she have?
3. Did a lot of girls swim at that time?
4. How do we know she was a talented swimmer?
5. Why was Trudy's Channel swim difficult?
6. How many extra kilometers did Trudy swim?
7. Did the men swim faster than Trudy?
8. What was Trudy's connection with swimming later in her life?

▶ Subskill: Writing in paragraphs

To help the reader understand, organize your writing into paragraphs. Each paragraph gives different information about the person.

3 Read descriptions a–f and choose the best one for each paragraph in the text. There are two you don't need.

- a Trudy at the Olympics
- b What Trudy did later
- c Trudy's swimming talent
- d Trudy's family
- e Trudy's Channel swim
- f When Trudy learned to swim

4 Read the text and complete the time expressions we use when describing actions in the past. Write one word in each space.

1. ________ 1905
2. ________ ________ ________ ________ 12
3. ________ ________ ________ 19
4. ________ her swim

5 **Write a biography of a person from history you admire. Follow the steps in the Skills boost**

SKILLS BOOST

THINK

1 Choose a person.

2 Use the internet to make notes about their life and what they did. Remember to check the information on more than one webpage.

New York – 1905 – Germany – 6 children
12: WSA – swimming not popular
8 world records, Olympic gold

PREPARE

Prepare a draft and organize your notes into logical paragraphs. For example: early life and family, how they got started, most important things they did, later life

WRITE

Write your biography. Use the example in exercise 1 to help you.

CHECK

Read your biography. Answer the questions.

1 Do you include interesting information about the person? ☐

2 Do you use simple past verbs correctly? ☐

3 Do you use past time expressions? ☐

4 Is your writing organized into logical paragraphs? ☐

6 **Peer review** **Read another student's biography. Is it interesting? Why?**

Quick review

Grammar

Simple past

Regular and irregular verbs

Some verbs are regular in the simple past.
They usually add *-ed*.

*She **started** school at nine o'clock.*

Other verbs are irregular and have different forms and spelling.

*He **had** lunch at 12:30.*

Common irregular verbs include:

come → came *do → did*
give → gave *go → went*
have → had *see → saw*

For a fuller list of irregular verbs, see pp134–135.

Negative and question forms

Form the negative: *didn't* (*did not*) + base form

*They **didn't do** their homework.*

Form *Yes/No* questions: *Did* (*you*) + base form?

Form short answers: *Yes,* (*I*) *did.*/*No,* (*I*) *didn't.*

Did** you **understand** the exercise?* *Yes, I **did.

Did** she **have** dinner with her family?* *No, she **didn't.

Past time expressions

Use time expressions to refer to the past:

*five years **ago***

***in** (2010)*

***when I was** eight*

***at the age of** nine*

Vocabulary

47 Jobs

accountant, actor, artist, businessman/woman, chef, dentist, doctor, engineer, journalist, lawyer, mechanic, nurse, photographer, pilot, police officer, receptionist, salesperson, scientist, singer, taxi driver, teacher, waiter, web designer

48 Adjectives to describe people

careful, careless, friendly, generous, kind, lazy, normal, polite, rude, special, talented, unfriendly, unkind

7 Project

WDYT?
(What do you think?)

What makes a hero?

TASK: Make a digital presentation about a hero from the past.

Learning outcomes

1 I can talk about a hero and say why they are important.

2 I can use feedback to improve my work.

3 I can use appropriate language from the unit.

Graphic organizer → Project planner p133

1 Watch a video of a student giving a presentation about a hero from the past. Why is Katherine Johnson a hero?

STEP 1: THINK

2 Read the slides in the Model project. Which questions do they answer?

1 Why is she a hero?
2 What was her job?
3 When was she born?
4 Who were the other people in her family?
5 What did she do?

3 Which of these things can you see?

- pictures
- questions
- long sentences
- facts and dates

STEP 2: PLAN

4 Work in pairs. Make a list of heroes. Think about people in science, sports, politics, literature, music, etc.

5 Individually, choose a hero. Make notes for your presentation. Use the presentation slides to help you.

STEP 3: CREATE

6 Read the *How to ...* tips on p133. Then create your digital presentation.

1 Give general information – who is this person? What did they do?
2 Give information about their early life.
3 Give information about their job/activities.
4 Say why you think they are a hero.

7 Work in pairs. Read the tips in the Super skills box and practice saying the Key phrases with a partner.

CREATIVITY — **SUPER SKILLS**

Using feedback to improve your work

Tips

Ask other students to help you.
Listen to their suggestions.
Change your work to make it better.

Key phrases

I really like the part about ...
How about including ... ?
Why don't you ... ?
This part is really clear.
What do you think about ... ?
I didn't really understand ...

8 Practice your presentation in groups. Use the tips and Key phrases in the Super skills box. What changes do other students suggest you make?

Model project

My hero from the past

1 Katherine Johnson

a math genius and scientist – 'the human computer'

worked at NASA

helped to send people into space

2 Her early life

1918 – born in West Virginia in the USA

1928 – started high school

went to university – studied math and French

became a teacher

3 Her work

1953 – started work at NASA

helped to send the first American into space

helped to send Apollo 11 to the Moon

4 Why is she a hero?

'Girls are capable of doing everything men are capable of doing.'

STEP 4: PRESENT

9 Present your digital presentation to the class.

10 Peer review Listen to your classmates and answer the questions.

1 Is the presentation clear and interesting?

2 Who is the most important hero from the past?

7 FINAL REFLECTION

1 The task

How well can you talk about the life of a hero from the past?

How well can you give a digital presentation?

2 Super skill

Can you listen to suggestions from your classmates and make changes? Give examples.

3 Language

Do you use language from the unit? Give examples.

8 Summer fun

WDYT?
(What do you think?)

What's your idea of a good vacation?

Vocabulary: vacations; vacation activities

Grammar: *will* for predictions; future with *going to*; present progressive for future arrangements

Reading: a travel blog about Virtual Reality vacations

Listening: phone conversations and messages about vacation plans

Speaking: making arrangements

Writing: invitations

Project: create a three-day vacation plan for you and your friends

Video skills p97

Real-world speaking p103

Project pp106–107

Vacations

1 **Look at the travel website. Match the types of vacations in the box with photos 1–7.**

> go **camping** go **hiking**
> go on a **water sports vacation** go **skiing**
> go to a **theme park resort** go to the **beach** go to the **city**

2 **Work in pairs. Tell your partner about your favorite and least favorite type of vacation. Explain why.**

3 **Match the sentences with the places in the box.**

> apartment B & B campsite
> country house hotel youth hostel

1 A really good one has five stars. ________
2 The letters in this name stand for 'Bed and Breakfast'. ________
3 If you stay here, you don't sleep in a bed or in a building. ________
4 This is a small house. It isn't in the city. ________
5 This place is only for you and your family. You can cook your own food there. ________
6 Here there are often a lot of beds in one room. ________

4 **For each vacation type in exercise 1, say one or more places to stay.**

5 **Work in pairs. Discuss the places you stay in when you go on vacation.**

Where do you stay?

We usually stay in an apartment at the beach.

6 **Match the facilities in the box to icons 1–7.**

bike rental   game room   gym   parking lot   picnic area   swimming pool   yard

7 **Read the descriptions and complete with places to stay and facilities.**

1 Last year we went camping at a ________ on Koh Kam Nui. There isn't a ________ , but that isn't important because it's next to the beach.

2 My cousin's wedding was in a small ________ in Monteverde. It was a sunny day and they got married in the ________ .

3 When we went to the city of Prague, we stayed in an ________ so we could make our own food. They offered ________ so we had a cheap way to travel around the city.

4 Last summer we went hiking near Banff and we stayed in a ________ with six people in each room because it was cheap. There wasn't a TV, but there was a ________ where you could play ping-pong.

VIDEO SKILLS

8 **Watch the video. What different holidays, or vacations, do you see?**

9 **Work in pairs. Discuss the questions.**

1 What is the main reason for this video?
   a to see the vlogger's vacation photos
   b to hear about different people's vacations
   c to sell a vacation
2 Who do you think would like this video?
3 What makes the video interesting? Think about: colors, photos, 360° effect, the presenter.

CELEBRITY CORNER

K-Pop band **BTS** made the 'See you in Seoul' video for tourists. Watch it on YouTube and find out what you can do there.

A travel blog

1 **Work in pairs. Read the vacation facts and discuss the questions.**

1 What type of vacation can you have in each place?
2 What facilities can you expect?
3 Which place would you most like to visit? Why?

Vacation facts

The world's most popular theme park is **The Magic Kingdom at Walt Disney World in Florida**, with more than an estimated 20 million visitors a year.

The world's most expensive hotel room is in **Geneva, Switzerland**. It costs around $80,000 a night!

The world's first space tourist paid $20 million to visit the **International Space Station**.

2 **Work in pairs. Look at the photos on p99 and answer the questions.**

1 What can you see in the photos?
2 What connects them?

3 **Read the introduction and the first paragraph of the text. Check your answers in exercise 2.**

4 49 **Read and listen to the text and circle the best summary.**

a There are lots of problems with traditional vacations.
b Virtual Reality will change how people buy and experience travel.
c People will stop traveling when we have VR.

5 **Are the sentences true or false? Find information in the text to support your answer.**

1 In the future, people will experience different places cheaply.
2 A travel company is using VR as an alternative vacation.
3 You can wear VR glasses in the ocean when swimming with dolphins.
4 People sitting in the same room will have the same VR experience.
5 A grandmother takes VR vacations because she has problems walking.

Subskill: Identifying facts and opinions

When you read, be careful to recognize the difference between fact and opinion. Adjectives like *amazing* and *terrible* and phrases like *I think* often indicate a personal opinion.

6 **Find the information in the text. Which sentences are fact and which are opinion?**

1 Virtual Reality travel is amazing.
2 A travel company now offers customers the chance to see their hotel using VR.
3 VR clothes help people feel as well as see.
4 VR shoes are fantastic.
5 A woman uses VR to visit destinations a long way from home.
6 VR glasses cost about $400.
7 VR glasses will get cheaper.

7 **Word work** **Match the definitions to the words in bold in the text.**

1 jump out of a plane with a large piece of material on your back ________
2 a place where water comes down from a high place ________
3 a very bad situation ________
4 a document you need for traveling to other countries ________
5 reserve (e.g. a restaurant or hotel) ________
6 walk up a hill or mountain ________

8 **Complete the sentences with words from exercise 7.**

1 You ________ 327 steps to the top of the tower.
2 We didn't ________ the restaurant and when we arrived there weren't any open tables.
3 When I lost my ________, I went to the police station.
4 Last year we visited the ________ in the Iguazu National Park.
5 I'm frightened of flying. If I had to ________ from a plane, it would be a ________ for me.

CRITICAL THINKING — SUPER SKILLS

1 **Remember** Which advantages of Virtual Reality travel does the text mention?
2 **Evaluate** Put the advantages in order of importance in your opinion.
3 What disadvantages can you see of VR vacations? Write a list.
4 **Create** Think of another activity that would be good to experience using Virtual Reality. Explain why.

Sit back, get comfortable and … TRAVEL?

This week on THE VACATION BLOG, I'm looking at how Virtual Reality (VR) could change all our ideas about vacations.

Would you like to **climb** Mount Everest? How about staying in a 5-star hotel or going skiing in New Zealand? If, like me, your answer is 'Yes, but…', don't worry. You will soon be able to do all this and it won't cost a lot of money. How? With amazing VR travel.

With VR, some of the things that can turn your perfect vacation into a **nightmare** simply disappear. One travel company recently started offering customers a virtual tour of their hotel. Can you see the swimming pool from your room? What's the game room like? Put on your VR glasses and take a look before you **book**.

With VR you can swim with dolphins, or **parachute** from a plane while the person next to you visits a **waterfall**. And soon the experience will be even better with special clothes to wear during your VR trip. With your VR shoes you will be able to see the water and feel it on your feet. Fantastic!

You don't need a **passport** or sunscreen, just your VR glasses. See you in Bali, or Alaska, or …

The Vacation Guy Comments (5) 10 Likes Share

COMMENTS

Lucien posted June 14 11:42 am
For me, food is the most important thing about a vacation. With VR you can visit Italy, but you can't eat pizza!

The Vacation Guy posted June 14 11:55 am
Good point, Lucien. But I'm sure we will eat VR food in the future!

Lucy Lake posted June 15 3:33 pm
VR travel is also good for people who can't walk well. I read about an 80-year-old grandmother who takes 3D vacations in Egypt, India and Australia.

Ryan posted June 15 6:16 pm
What will this cost? Will it be expensive?

The Vacation Guy posted June 15 6:33 pm
No, it won't! VR glasses cost about $400 and I'm sure they'll get cheaper soon.

will for predictions: affirmative and negative

1 Complete the table with the examples.

We **will eat** VR food in the future.
It **won't cost** a lot of money.

Affirmative and negative			
subject	***will/won't***	**verb**	
People 1	will	have	vacations in space.
We 2	won't	need	a passport.

2 Complete the predictions with the affirmative or negative form of the verb in parentheses.

Ten years from now, ...

1 people ________ **(have +)** vacations on Mars.
2 we ________ **(need -)** passports. We ________ **(have +)** an ID microchip.
3 we ________ **(take -)** money on vacation. We ________ **(use +)** virtual money.
4 we ________ **(use +)** our phones to translate what people say when we're on vacation.

will for predictions: questions and short answers

3 Complete the tables with the examples.

What will this cost?
Will it be expensive? No, it **won't**.

Questions	Short answers		
Will we visit the Moon? 1	Yes, we **will**. 2		
***Wh-* questions**			
Question word	***will***	**subject**	**verb**
Where 3	will	we	travel?

4 Work in pairs. Read the predictions in exercise 2 again. Do you agree with them?

Will people take vacations on Mars?

No, they won't. Not in ten years.

5 Order the words to make questions.

1 speak to next / Who / on the phone / will / you ?
2 be like / tomorrow / What / the weather / will ?
3 you / go / tonight / What time / will / to bed ?
4 when you / What job / leave school / will / have / you ?

6 Work in pairs. Ask and answer the questions in exercise 5.

7 Complete the text with the correct form of the verbs in the box.

become have look take travel (x2)

How will vacations change?

2030 According to a recent report, underwater hotels **1** ________ **(+)** more popular, but if you don't like that idea, your computer **2** ________ **(+)** at your online activity and suggest places to visit.

2050 Flying will be very different: airplanes **3** ________ **(+)** 360° windows. One question many people want to know is: **4** ________ **(we/?)** in space? The answer is yes, but not only to visit other planets. Planes will fly much higher and it **5** ________ **(-)** more than two and a half hours to fly from London to Sydney.

2100 Vacations will certainly be very different, but **6** ________ **(we/how/?)** Forget trains, planes and cars: Mary Jacquiline Romero, an expert from the University of Glasgow, predicts we will travel by teleportation!

8 Answer the question to solve the Brain teaser.

BRAIN TEASER

Look at the three diagrams.

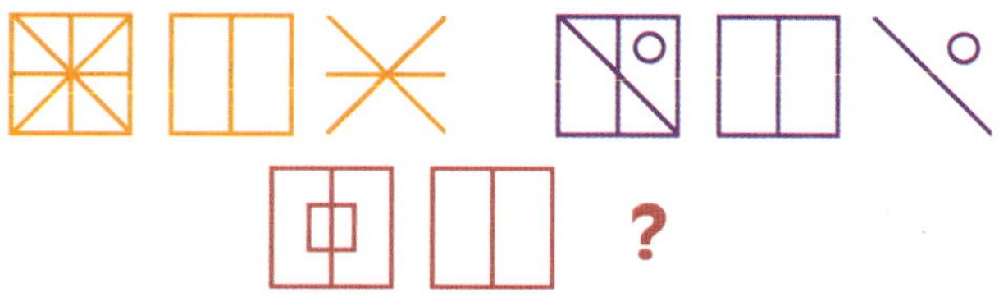

What will the final picture be in the last one?

Pronunciation: *will* p129
Reinforcement and Challenge Grammar bootcamp pp126–127

Vacation activities

1 **Read the blog. What activities can you see in the photos?**

Awesome things to do over summer break!

In this week's blog, we look at some great ways to spend a 'staycation'.

1 Be a tourist at home

Perhaps you can't go on vacation but you can be a tourist in your town. **Go sightseeing** and visit places of interest. **Go on a bus tour** or just walk around.

2 Get wet!

Spend a day at the swimming pool or go to a water park. Better still, **go on a day trip** to the beach and swim in the ocean.

3 Spend time outside

Go for a bike ride every day or **go for a walk** in the park. When it's sunny, take a book or music and sunbathe. Don't forget your sunglasses!

4 Make mealtimes special

Go for a pizza with friends at a local pizzeria or invite them to your house and have a barbecue at home.

5 Enjoy the arts

Find out what's going on in your town during summer break. Visit a museum or an art gallery. If you prefer live music, go to a concert.

6 Help out

Don't just **hang out with friends** all summer, do something useful. Volunteer for a local charity or offer to take care of neighbors' pets.

7 Organize visits

Take time to visit family – aunts, uncles and cousins. Arrange to **stay with a friend** or invite them to stay with you.

2 **Match the definitions to some of the phrases in bold in the blog.**

1 eat pizza in a restaurant
2 visit a place for a day
3 spend time with friends
4 visit interesting places in a town or city
5 sleep at a friend's house
6 walk for fun
7 lie in the sun

3 **Complete the phrases with the correct words from the blog.**

1 ________________ a bus tour/a day trip
2 ________________ a water park/a concert
3 ________________ a bike ride/a walk/a pizza

4 **Work in pairs. What do you think are the three best ideas in the blog? Why?**

Phone conversations and messages

5 50 **Listen to six people expressing how they're feeling. Match the words in the box to the speakers.**

bored confused excited nervous sad surprised

Subskill: Listening for feelings

To identify a speaker's feelings, listen to words and intonation.

6 51 **Listen to three speakers on the phone. How is each speaker feeling?**

a Sam b Nina c Ed

7 **Listen again. In which extract does a speaker talk about a plan to … ?**

1 go for a walk ________
2 go to a water park ________
3 take care of a younger sister ________
4 hang out with a friend ________
5 meet on the weekend ________

8 **Listen again and answer the questions.**

1 When and where do Sam and Alisha plan to meet? ________________
2 When is the music festival? ________________
3 When does Lily plan to buy tickets? ________________
4 When does Ed want to meet his friend? ________________
5 What two activities does he say that they can do? ________________

9 **Work in pairs. Answer the questions.**

1 How long are the school breaks in your country? (How many weeks?)
2 Do you ever feel bored during summer vacation? Why/Why not?
3 What do you think is the ideal number of weeks for summer vacation?

Future with *going to*

1 **Read the examples and complete the rule.**

Affirmative
I'**m going to** buy tickets tomorrow.
She'**s going to** take care of her sister.
They'**re going to** try the new water slide.
Negative
I'**m not going to** take a vacation this year.
He **isn't going to** see his friends.
They **aren't going to** be home until late.

To talk about future plans and intentions, use:
subject + ________ (*not*) + *going to* + ________ .

2 **Complete the sentences with *going to* and the verb in parentheses.**

1 I ________ **(study)** for exams next weekend.
2 My mom ________ **(not work)** on Saturday.
3 My parents ________ **(go)** shopping.
4 A friend ________ **(come)** to my place to play games.
5 I ________ **(not watch)** TV.

3 **Change the sentences in exercise 2 to make them true for you about next weekend.**

I'm not going to study for exams next weekend. I'm going to hang out with friends.

4 **Complete the table with *is*, *are*, *isn't* or *aren't*.**

Questions	Short answers
Are you **going to** be at home this afternoon?	Yes, I **am**. No, I'**m not**.
1 ________ she **going to** go to the concert?	Yes, she **is**. No, she 2 ________ .
3 ________ they **going to** play games?	Yes, they **are**. No, they 4 ________ .

5 **Order the words to make questions.**

1 vacation / go / going / on / Are / you / to ?
____
2 going / Where / to / you / go / are ?
____
3 stay / to / are / you / Where / going ?
____
4 to / you / going / on / go / Are / any day trips ?
____

6 **Work in pairs. Ask and answer the questions in exercise 5.**

Present progressive for future arrangements

7 **Read the examples and circle the correct option in the rule.**

We'**re meeting** at the bus station at 8:00.
A band **is playing** in the park on Saturday.
What **are** you **doing** this afternoon?

We use the present progressive to talk about **possible/definite** arrangements in the future.

8 **Read Marco's calendar and write sentences about his plans for the week.**

Monday	meet Liam 1:00
Tuesday	have a guitar lesson 5:30
Wednesday	take a bus to the water park 8:00
Thursday	go to the movies with Izan 7:00
Friday	stay with Adrian
Saturday	travel to the mountains

On Monday, he's meeting Liam at one o'clock.

9 **Circle the correct option.**

GRAMMAR ROUND-UP
1 2 3 4 5 6 7 8

Why not try geocaching this summer?

I **1 discover/'m discovering/discovered** geocaching two years **2 before/ago/past**. The idea is simple. You go to the geocaching website, and it **3 give/is giving/gives** you the location of a box. You use the GPS on your phone to find it.

There **4 is/are/was** objects in the box. You take one, but you **5 can/can't/must** put another object back into the box – those are the rules of the game!

The last time I went geocaching, for example, there **6 is/was/were** a key ring. I **7 take/'m taking/took** it and put in some pens.

This summer, I **8 will/going to/'m going to** do it again. I love being in the countryside, and this is **9 good/better/best** than going for a walk. Try it, you **10 love/are loving/will love** it!

Research

Where can you go geocaching in your country?

Reinforcement and Challenge Grammar bootcamp p127

Making arrangements

1 **Work in pairs. Talk about your plans for next weekend.**

2 **Watch the video and answer the questions.**

1 What do Maria and Sam decide to do?

2 When and where are they going to meet?

3 **Watch again. Which Key phrases do you hear?**

4 **Complete the dialogue with the Key phrases. Watch again and check.**

Maria: Hey, why don't we go for a bike ride this weekend?

Sam: Great idea! When?

Maria: How about Saturday morning?

Sam: **1** _________ Saturday morning. I'm going to the dentist.

Maria: Poor you! **2** _________ in the afternoon?

Sam: **3** _________ , I'm going to help my dad. We're having a barbecue to celebrate my exam results. **4** _________ anything Sunday?

Maria: I'm playing tennis in the morning, but **5** _________ in the afternoon.

Sam: Me, too.

Maria: OK, let's meet at the park at 2:30.

Sam: Awesome!

5 **Create your own dialogue. Follow the steps in the Skills boost.**

SKILLS BOOST

THINK

Individually, make a calendar of a week. Write activities in the calendar. Leave two days free.

PREPARE

Prepare a dialogue. Choose an activity you both want to do, and decide when you can do it.

PRACTICE

Practice your dialogue.

PERFORM

Act out your dialogue for the class.

6 **Peer review** **Listen to your classmates and answer the questions.**

1 What do they decide to do and when do they decide to do it?

2 How many Key phrases do they use?

Key phrases

What are you doing Saturday?
What are you up to Saturday?
Nothing special. Why?
I can't Saturday morning. I'm ...
Are you free in the afternoon?
How about Saturday morning?
Yes, I think so. / No, sorry, I'm ...
Are you doing anything Sunday?
I'm busy Sunday morning.
I'm free in the afternoon.

US → UK

Let's meet at two thirty. (US) → Let's meet at half past two. (UK)

Invitations

1 **Match the emojis with the meanings.**

a party bike Bye! camping happy sad

1 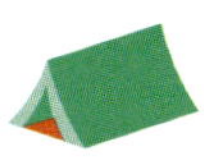

2 

3 

4 

5 

6 

2 **Read the messages. Who is going ... ?**

1 camping on the weekend ________
2 for a bike ride on Monday ________

3 **Answer the questions.**

1 When is Ian leaving to go camping?
2 Why can't Emma go for a bike ride on Monday afternoon?
3 What time is Jake meeting Emma?
4 Where are they meeting?
5 What is Jake doing on Sunday?

4 **Read the messages again. Find three phrases for inviting and five phrases for responding.**

Inviting	Responding ('yes')	Responding ('no')
Would you like to come?		

5 **Complete the messages with phrases for inviting and responding.**

Amy: Hi, Josh! Do **1** ________ go to the movies?
Josh: I **2** ________ to. When?
Amy: On Saturday evening.
Josh: Sorry, **3** ________. I'm going for a with Sean. Would you **4** ________ come?
Amy: OK, **5** ________ fun.

▶ Subskill: Apostrophes

We use apostrophes to show possession (*my mom's car*) or with contractions (*That's (is) great!*).

6 **Find examples of apostrophes in the messages ...**

1 with a singular noun to show possession
2 with a plural noun to show possession
3 to substitute a letter or letters in a word (contraction)

7 **Add the missing apostrophes in each sentence.**

1 Its hot today so Im going to the park.
2 Id love to come, but I have a guitar lesson.
3 Sorry, we cant. Were going for a pizza.
4 My parents anniversary is on Saturday and theyre having a party.

8 **Write a message dialogue. Follow the steps in the Skills boost.**

SKILLS BOOST

THINK

1 Think of a place you want to go to, or an activity you want to do.

____

2 Choose a day and a time to do this.

____

PREPARE

Make notes for your messages. Include an invitation (Person A) and a reply (Person B).

Person A	Person B
1 Ask about plans	2 Say you aren't sure
3 Make an invitation	4 Say 'no', and why
5 Make a second invitation	6 Say 'yes'
7 Arrange where and when to meet	

WRITE

Write your message dialogue.

CHECK

Read your description. Answer the questions.

1 Do you use *going to* for plans/intentions, and the present progressive for future arrangements? ☐
2 Do you use phrases for inviting and replying? ☐
3 Do you use apostrophes correctly? ☐

9 **Peer review** **Exchange your messages with another student. What does the writer decide to do and when?**

Quick review

Grammar

will for predictions

To make predictions about the future, use: *will/won't* + base form

*Airplanes **will be** bigger and faster.*
*People **won't travel** by train or car.*

To make questions, use: (Question word) + *will* + subject + base form

Will** people **go** on vacations in 2050? Yes, they **will.**/No, they **won't.
*What **will** it cost?*

Future with *going to*

To talk about future plans and intentions, use *going to.*
subject + *be* (*not*) + *going to* + base form

*Nina **isn't going to go** to the concert.*
*They're **going to meet** and play games.*

To make questions with *going to*, use:
(Question word) + *be* + subject + base form

*What **are** you **going to do** this summer?*
Are** you **going to go** on vacation? Yes, I **am.**/No, I'm **not.

Present progressive for future arrangements

To talk about future arrangements, use the present progressive.

*We're **meeting** at the bus station at 8:00.*
*We **aren't going** on vacation this year.*
*What **are** you **doing** on Saturday?*

Vocabulary

52 Types of vacation

go camping, go hiking, go on a water sports vacation, go skiing, go to a theme park resort, go to the beach, go to the city

53 Places to stay

apartment, B & B, campsite, country house, hotel, youth hostel

54 Facilities

bike rental, game room, gym, parking lot, picnic area, swimming pool, yard

55 Vacation activities

go for a bike ride, go for a pizza, go for a walk, go on a bus tour, go on a day trip, go sightseeing, go to a concert, go to a water park, hang out with friends, have a barbecue, stay with a friend, sunbathe, take care of a pet, visit a museum or art gallery, visit family

8 Project

WDYT?
(What do you think?)

What's your idea of a good vacation?

TASK: Create a three-day vacation plan for you and your friends.

Learning outcomes

1 I can plan a trip and present ideas clearly.
2 I can communicate my opinions in a group discussion.
3 I can use appropriate language from the unit.

Graphic organizer → Project planner p133

1 Watch a video of students practicing their presentation. Where do they want to go?

STEP 1: THINK

2 Look at the vacation plan in the Model project. What information does it include?

- how much things cost
- exact time of activities
- type of accommodation
- ideas for meals
- plans for activities and places to visit
- things to pack

3 Would you like to go on this trip? Why/Why not?

STEP 2: PLAN

4 Work in groups. Read the tips in the Super skills box and practice saying the Key phrases with your group.

COMMUNICATION — SUPER SKILLS

Communicating clearly

Tips

Look at your classmates when you speak.
When you give an opinion, give reasons why.
Make sure all your classmates agree.
Make sure everyone participates fully in the discussion.

Key phrases

I think this is a good idea because ...
Do we all agree?
You're very quiet. What do you think?
What do you think is best?
I think this is the best option because ...
I don't think that's a good idea because ...

5 Work in groups of three. Choose a place to visit for a three-day vacation. Use the tips and Key phrases in the Super skills box. Consider:

- the type of accommodation you can stay in
- places to visit and activities you can do there; include at least one cultural activity and one outdoor activity
- a mix of places that are interesting for everyone in the group
- different types of food for different meals
- a trip that won't be too expensive

STEP 3: CREATE

6 Choose a format and create your presentation.

7 Agree how you are going to present your plan. Read the *How to ...* tips on p133 and practice your presentation.

Model project

PLAN: *three-day vacation in Glasgow*

Tues 14th
Travel to Glasgow
Arrive at B & B
Dinner: burger

Wed 15th
Breakfast: B & B
Morning at Science Center
Lunch: packed lunch
Afternoon at movie theater
Dinner: pizza

Thurs 16th
Breakfast: B & B
Visit Riverside Museum
Travel home

STEP 4: PRESENT

8 Peer review **Present your plan to another group. As you listen to your classmates, think about the questions.**

1 Would you like to go on this vacation?
2 Is the information presented well?
3 Think of a question about the vacation plans.

8 FINAL REFLECTION

1 The task

Is the plan well prepared, with activities for different types of people?

Is the information clear and well presented?

2 Super skill

Does everyone communicate their ideas well in the group?

3 Language

Do you use language from the unit? Give examples.

REVIEW

Look what you know!

Vocabulary

1 **Name the things you can see in the photos.**

2 **For each word in exercise 1, write the letter indicated.**

A	B	C	D	E	F	G	H	I
4th letter	5th letter	2nd letter	4th letter	3rd letter	2nd letter	1st letter	5th letter	1st letter
G								

3 **Which word/phrase does not go with the verb in bold?**

1 **go** home to school ~~soccer~~ skiing
2 **do** your homework karate yoga breakfast
3 **play** in a band gymnastics hockey on a team
4 **start** school at 8:00 a business a new club home
5 **go** badminton to the city sightseeing to bed
6 **stay** at home sad in a youth hostel with a friend
7 **take** a break social media a shower photos

4 **Choose the correct verb for the odd one out in exercise 3.**

play soccer

5 **Work in pairs. Complete the questions using phrases from exercise 4. Then ask and answer.**

1 When do you ________________ ?
2 Do you know anyone who ________________ ?
3 What time do you ________________ after school?
4 Can you ________________ at your school?
5 What do you do when you ________________ ?
6 How often do you ________________ ?

6 **Match 1–12 with a–l to make compounds.**

1	bus	a	bag
2	country	b	trip
3	day	c	house
4	game	d	cream
5	horseback	e	driver
6	ice	f	park
7	department	g	pool
8	sleeping	h	riding
9	swimming	i	room
10	ping-	j	store
11	taxi	k	station
12	theme	l	pong

7 **Complete the description with words from exercise 6.**

Last year I went on vacation with my cousins. We stayed in a **1** ________ in Cancun. They had a **2** ________ where we could play **3** ________ . There was also a **4** ________ , and the water was really warm!

One day, we went on a **5** ________ to an amazing **6** ________ . My cousin Javi ate too much **7** ________ and felt very bad on one of the rides!

I traveled home before my cousins. My aunt took me to the **8** ________ , but at first we couldn't find it. In the end, a **9** ________ told us where to go.

Reading

1 **Match 1–3 with a–c to make sentences. They give advice from the Subskills in Units 1–8.**

1 Look at photos and the title of a text before ...
2 The first time you read a text, read quickly to get ...
3 To find specific information, ...
a first identify key words in the exercise that will help you.
b reading it to help you understand what it's about.
c a general idea of what it's about.

Reading tip

Use the advice in exercise 1 to help you with the reading tasks on this page.

2 **Look at the texts on this page but don't read them! Where are they from? How do you know?**

a a live feed b a book c a newspaper

3 **Read the titles of the stories. With a partner predict three items of vocabulary you think are in each story.**

a A place of extremes
b No more boys and girls
c Vacation essentials
d The best place to live

4 56 **Read and listen to the stories. Match the titles in exercise 3 with each story.**

5 **Are the sentences true or false?**

1 John Lewis stopped selling children's clothes.
2 One problem was the typical color of girls' clothes.
3 Atacama is dry because of its position.
4 There's rain in all parts of the Atacama desert, but only a little.
5 Bristol is not a good place for biking.
6 London isn't a very healthy city.
7 Over half of British people take food on vacation.
8 They take food because they can't ask for things in another language.

6 **Correct the false sentences in exercise 5.**

Exam tip

If a question has several parts, make sure you leave time to do all of them. If you don't try a question you won't get any points.

7 **Word work** **The words in bold in the text all appeared in the Word work exercises in Units 1–8. Can you remember what they mean?**

8 **Work in pairs. Order the stories from most to least interesting, then compare your order with your partner. If it's different, explain your reasons.**

1 ________

Striped leggings, a top with dinosaurs, cool sneakers – but are these great kids' clothes for boys or girls? At John Lewis department stores now, there isn't a difference. They didn't like the idea of pink clothes for girls, or boys' clothes with words like 'Future Scientist' so they decided to stop having separate sections for boys' and girls' clothes and just sell a **mix** of clothes for all children.

2 ________

The Atacama in Chile is officially the driest **desert** on Earth. The **average** rainfall is just 1 mm and in parts of the desert, it never rains. Its position between the Andes mountains and the ocean means that rain clouds often can't get to the Atacama. Experts think the last time it rained in some places was hundreds of years ago.

3 ________

Britain's healthiest town is Bristol! With 45 sports clubs and more than 230 bicycle routes, the **citizens** of Bristol live in the top place for a healthy life. Experts counted swimming pools, parks, sports centers and fast-food restaurants. What about London? It was number 5 – from the bottom!

Source: SBO.net

4 ________

What do more than 60% of British people take when they go on vacation? Is it sunscreen, a guidebook, or a toothbrush? You're wrong! The answer is quite strange! Among the things British people pack, one of the most important is food. Some people don't like foreign food and drinks; others think it's too expensive. Among the most popular things you can find in a British suitcase are tea and instant coffee, cookies and noodles!

Grammar

The questions around the edge of the page will help you remember the grammar studied in the book. First answer the red questions around the page. Next, do the exercises in the central red section. Then do the same with green, blue and yellow.

20 Complete the sentence: *When I get home from school later today, I (...) do my homework.*

19 How do you write this sentence in the past? *Einstein is a famous scientist.*

The red sections focus on possessive adjectives and object pronouns, simple present, adverbs of frequency and *love, like, hate.*

1 Complete the sentences with a possessive adjective or object pronoun.

1 (you) Is that *your* pen?
2 (he) That's Alan. I sit with ____ in history.
3 (they) Oh – eggs! Sorry, I don't like ____ .
4 (she) Look at that girl! I love ____ jacket!
5 (we) Mr. Anand is ____ math teacher.
6 (we) Joel lives on the same street as ____ .
7 (I) Can you help ____ , please?

2 Circle the correct option.

1 My brother **studies/study** computer science.
2 Where **does/do** your grandparents live?
3 My dad **don't/doesn't** work in an office.
4 Do you like **play/playing** computer games?
5 We never **watch/watches** TV.
6 My brother **is always/always is** late.
7 I sometimes **listen/listening** to music.

3 Complete the sentences with the words in parentheses.

1 A: What languages (...) **(you/speak)**?
B: I (...) **(speak)** Turkish and a little German.
2 A: (...) **(your brother/play)** any sports?
B: Yes, he (...) **(do)**. He (...) **(go)** swimming.
3 A: What hobbies (...) **(your parents/have)**?
B: My dad (...) **(take)** photos, but my mom (...) **(not have)** much free time.
4 A: What time (...) **(your sister/get up)**?
B: At 6 am. She often (...) **(study)** before school.

18 *You mustn't be late!* Is it OK to be late?

17 What form of a verb do you use after *like, love* and *hate*?

The green sections focus on the present progressive, comparatives and superlatives, and modals of obligation, permission and prohibition.

1 Write the verbs in the simple present or present progressive.

Ben: Hi Josh. What **1** (...) **(you/do)** right now?
Josh: I **2** (...) **(walk)** to the sports center. I always **3** (...) **(play)** basketball on Mondays. What about you?
Ben: Dad **4** (...) **(make)** dinner and I **5** (...) **(help)** him.
Josh: **6** (...) **(your dad/always/cook)**?
Ben: Only when he **7** (...) **(get)** home early.

2 Complete the questions with the comparative or superlative adjectives. Then ask a partner.

1 What is the (...) **(easy)** school subject?
2 Which is (...) **(difficult)** to learn, English or Japanese?
3 What is the (...) **(big)** store in your town?
4 What is the (...) **(bad)** program on TV? Why?
5 Which is (...) **(good)**, pizza or ice cream?

3 Complete the school rules with *can, can't, must* or *mustn't*. Which rules do you have in your school?

1 Listen when others are speaking.
You must listen when others are speaking.
2 Don't use your cell phone in class.
3 It's OK to write on the board.
4 Bring your books to class.
5 Don't talk in class.
6 It's OK to wear sneakers.
7 No eating in the classroom.

16 Make two predictions about your life in 2035.

15 What is the difference between *How much ... ?* and *How many ... ?*

14 What is the superlative form of the adjective *hot*?

13 Do adverbs of frequency (*always, sometimes, never*) come before or after the verb *be*?

1 Complete the list: me, you, (...) , (...) , it, (...) , you, (...)

2 Complete the sentence: *Right now, I'm ...*

3 Add two more words in each category. Countable nouns: *tomatoes*, (...) , (...) . Uncountable nouns: *rice*, (...) , (...) .

4 What do you add to regular verbs to make the simple past?

The blue sections focus on countable and uncountable nouns, *there is/are*, *some*, *any*, *much*, *many* and the simple past form of *be*.

1 Correct the mistake in each sentence.

1 Would you like a apple or a banana?
2 There are any great stores in town.
3 Is there some library near here?
4 There isn't some chocolate in the cake.
5 Are there any ice cream in the fridge?
6 I usually have a sandwich and a milk for breakfast.

2 Write questions for these answers using *How much ... ?* or *How many ... ?*

1 I play two sports: hockey and tennis.
2 I have $20 in my pocket.
3 I have two sisters.
4 I usually spend an hour a day on homework.
5 I eat an apple and a banana every day.
6 I usually read a book every month.

3 Complete the dialogue with *was/wasn't*, *were/weren't*, *there was/wasn't*, *there were/weren't* or *was/were there*.

Jamie: Hey, why **1** (...) you late for class this morning?
Carla: I **2** (...) at Levi's birthday party last night.
Jamie: Oh, right. **3** (...) a lot of people there?
Carla: Yes, **4** (...), and **5** (...) music and dancing.
Jamie: **6** (...) any food?
Carla: No, **7** (...) , but **8** (...) a cake.

5 Rewrite the sentence in the negative form: *He gets up at seven o'clock.*

6 *She's playing tennis.* What do we call this tense? When do we use it?

The yellow sections focus on the past simple and look at future forms.

1 Rewrite the sentences in the affirmative, negative or question form.

1 He came to school by car today. **(?)**
Did he come to school by car today?
2 I didn't go to bed early last night. **(+)**
3 Did she help you with your homework? **(-)**
4 They took a picnic with them. **(?)**
5 Did the class start at 9:00? **(+)**
6 He didn't call me on the weekend. **(?)**
7 They gave me their address. **(-)**

2 Write questions for the answers about Angus's evening out.

1 He went to the movie theater.
What did Angus do last night?
2 He saw an adventure movie.
3 He went with Kate.
4 It cost $8.
5 They sat in the front row.
6 It started at 7:30.

3 Circle the correct option.

1 **Will you go/Are you going** to the park after school?
2 **I'm going to buy/I'll buy** a new game this weekend.
3 People **will have/are having** vacations on Mars in 2050.
4 People **won't use/aren't using** money in the future.
5 We **aren't going to/won't** stay at home this summer.

7 Circle the correct option: There *is/are* three museums near my home.

8 What is the simple past of these irregular verbs? *go, meet, see, come, write*

9 Order the words to make a question: *do / go / Where / they / to school ?*

10 Write the comparative form of these adjectives: *tall, interesting.* What's the rule?

11 Complete the sentence: *We don't have (...) milk.*

12 What is the question? *We went to the movie theater last night.*

Listening

1 **Work in pairs. Answer the questions.**

1. Where and when do you listen to music?
2. How do you listen (using a cell phone, with headphones, etc.)?
3. Do you ever listen to podcasts? Which ones?
   - science
   - sports
   - history
   - other

2 **Look at the podcasts. What is each one about? Write three words you expect to hear in each program.**

Remember

Use key words to help you understand.

3 57 **Listen to the extracts. Which five podcasts do you hear? Write the order 1–5.**

4 **Listen again. Answer the questions.**

1. What ingredients do you need to make the chocolate cake?
2. Where will people have vacations in ten years' time?
3. What extreme weather happened last night?
4. What do the people do with their clothes?
5. What was special about the giant tortoise?

5 **Work in pairs. Answer the questions.**

1. Which podcasts do you think are interesting? Why?
2. Which one would you choose to listen to?

6 **Look at the photo. What can you see? What do you know about these events?**

7 58 **Listen to a podcast about e-sports. Circle the correct answer (a–c).**

Exam tip

Take time to read the questions before you listen.

1. Why does the speaker think e-sports are real sports?
   - **a** Players must run and do exercise.
   - **b** It's important to eat healthy food.
   - **c** Players practice to be good at the game.
2. Why did e-sports start?
   - **a** Technology became better.
   - **b** More people wanted to play video games.
   - **c** It was possible to watch games online.
3. In what ways are e-sports more than a hobby?
   - **a** Players spend millions of dollars on games.
   - **b** Traditional soccer teams have e-players.
   - **c** There's a world organization for e-sports.
4. What does he think about e-sports at school?
   - **a** Schools will have e-sports teams in the future.
   - **b** They're good for students who can't play traditional sports.
   - **c** It's a good idea to have video games at sports day.
5. What is his opinion about the future of e-sports?
   - **a** They will be more popular than traditional sports.
   - **b** There will be more e-sports programs on TV.
   - **c** People won't play soccer, only video games.

8 **Listen again and check your answers.**

9 **Work in pairs. Name one thing about e-sports that ...**

- you already knew
- you didn't know before
- you were surprised about

Real-world speaking

1 **Works in pairs. Look at the photos.**

1 What is the situation in each photo?

2 What other situations did you learn about on the Real-world speaking pages?

2 **Copy and complete the table with the Key phrases in the box.**

Key phrases

How much is it?
What time does it start?
Is there a subway station near here?
Are you free on Saturday?
What do you think of hip hop music?
Why don't we take a picnic?

Asking for information	Shopping for clothes	Making suggestions
Asking for directions	**Giving opinions**	**Making arrangements**

3 **Add two more phrases in each category.**

4 **Circle the correct option.**

I'd like to **1 find out/find** about the gym, please.

Of course.

Have you got a karate class?

Yes, we have.

What day is it **2 at/on**?

Mondays, from 7 to 9.

Can I **3 sign up/look** for it?

Yes, of course.

Can I **4 try/put** these sneakers on, please?

Sure.

They look good, but they're a bit small.

What **5 size/type** are they?

7. Do you have them in an 8?

Yes, here you are.

Oh, these are better. I'll **6 take/buy** them.

5 **Work in pairs. Create a dialogue for one of these situations. Follow the steps in the Skills boost.**

A Make an arrangement to do something together this weekend.
Discuss when you are free. You like different things, but decide what to do and when to do it.

B You're shopping. You want to buy a present for a friend's birthday.
Make suggestions about what to buy (you have different ideas). Make a decision.

C Talk about a course or hobby that you started recently.
Ask and answer questions about where and when you do it. Talk about your experience and show interest!

SKILLS BOOST

THINK
Choose a situation.

PREPARE
Write your dialogue. Include four Key phrases.

PRACTICE
Practice your dialogue. Try to remember it.

PERFORM
Act out your dialogue for the class.

Exam tip
Try to stay calm in speaking exams. Take deep breaths before you start.

6 **Peer review** **Listen to your classmates and answer the questions.**

1 Which task did they choose?

2 Which Key phrases did they use?

Writing

1 **Read the texts quickly. Match text types 1–5 with examples A–E.**

1 a blog ____ 2 an invitation ____ 3 an email ____ 4 instructions ____ 5 a forum post ____

A **Molly**

Hi Molly,

How was your vacation? I went to the north of France. We stayed in a cottage and went walking every day. It was beautiful, but the weather wasn't good …

B

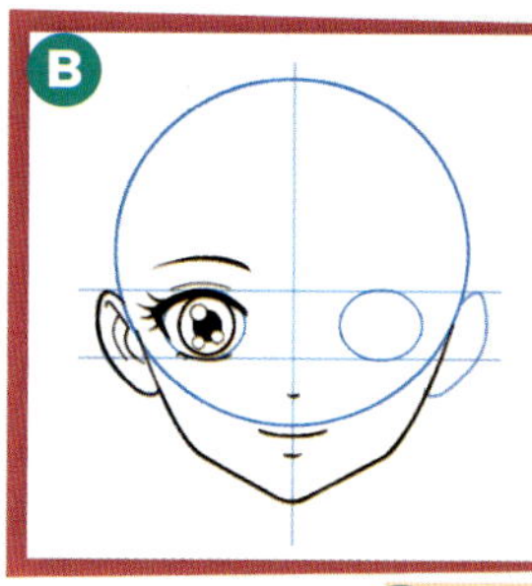

First of all, draw a circle. ➡ *Then add two circles for the eyes.* ➡ *Remember, in animé, the eyes are always big …*

C

| ABOUT | BLOG | CONTACT

My Diary

Posted by Lee 13th June

This week our class did a project about animals. We could talk about endangered animals or animals that were extinct …

D

Hi Abby!

Hi! How are things?

Good, thanks. I'm going shopping this afternoon. Do you want to come?

Sure! Can Fran come too?

E

| Register | FAQ | New Posts | Community |

What are the typical dishes in your country?

Hi, I'm from Italy. Italian food is famous all over the world because it's really good! Our most popular dishes are pasta (in my region we cook it with pesto, a green sauce) …

2 **Find the words or phrases in the texts and answer the questions. You have five minutes!**

1 *First of all, Then …*
Write three more words to order events. **(Unit 6)**

2 two countries with capital letters
Name four rules for capital letters. **(Unit 1)**

3 *and, but, or*
Which do we use to add … ? **(Unit 2)**
a a different idea
b a similar idea
c an alternative

4 an adjective to describe a place
Write three other adjectives to describe places. **(Unit 5)**

5 *too*
What other words do we use to add information? What is the position of these words in a sentence? **(Unit 4)**

6 *because*
What is the difference between because and so? **(Unit 3)**

3 **Correct the sentences.**

1 I went swimming and I played volleyball also.
2 We have math on mondays.
3 There are lots of interestings things to do here.
4 Do you prefer quiet and busy places?
5 We stayed in a town small in spain last august.

4 **Choose one task and write your answer in 120 words. Follow the steps in the Skills boost.**

A Write a blog about your last vacation.
Describe the weather, where you stayed and what you did. What was the best thing about it?

B Write an email to a friend.
Tell him/her about your plans for the summer.

C You see this post online. Write your answer.
I want to visit new places, but I don't know where! Tell me about your town. What can I do there?

SKILLS BOOST

THINK
Make notes about the information to include.

PREPARE
Organize your writing into paragraphs.

WRITE
Write your blog, email or online post.

CHECK
Check your writing for tenses, vocabulary, punctuation and linking words (because, but, etc.).

5 **Peer review** **Exchange your writing with other students. Answer the questions.**

1 Which task did they do?
2 Are the tenses, vocabulary, punctuation and linking words correct?

REVIEW GAME

How to play the REVIEW GAME

1 Form groups of three to five students.
2 Each student needs a different coin or marker. Put these on START.
3 In turn, roll a dice, move forward and do what it says on the square.
4 The winner is the first to FINISH!

Key phrases:
You start.
Whose turn is it?
What's the question?
It's your/my turn.

START

1 Ask someone in your group for directions to a place in your town.

2 Talk about what you eat on a typical day.

3 You have one minute. How many objects in the classroom can you name?

4 Miss a turn

5 Compare your city with another place in your country.

6 Describe what someone in your group is wearing.

7 Go back three squares

8 Make arrangements to meet someone in your group next weekend.

9 Talk about the rules in your ideal school.

10 Speak for one minute about 'My last birthday'.

11 Describe your typical day.

12 Go forward two squares

13 Tell the group about one of your heroes.

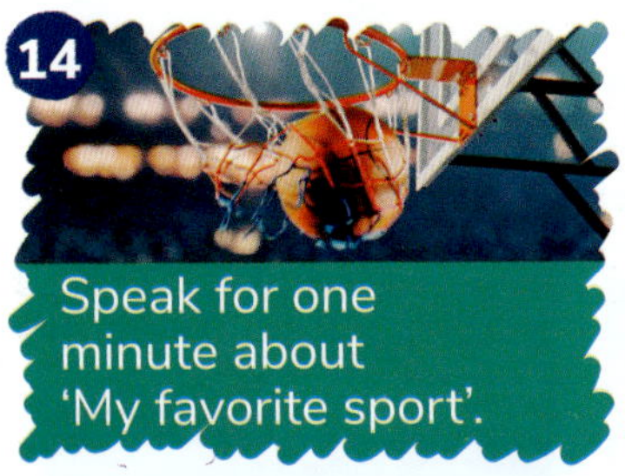

14 Speak for one minute about 'My favorite sport'.

15 Say what you did last weekend.

16 Say four things you can take on a trip.

17 Miss a turn

18 Speak for one minute about 'My plans for my vacation'.

19 Go back to START

20 You have one minute. How many animals can you name?

21 Describe the weather in your country at different times of the year.

FINISH

Grammar bootcamp

Starter unit

be: affirmative and negative

1 Write the contracted forms of the verb.

1 I am not Mexican. *I'm not*
2 He is a musician. _____
3 They are in my class. _____
4 We are not brothers. _____
5 You are in the basketball team. _____
6 She is not 14. She is 13. _____
7 It is a red book. _____

2 Look at the photo and write complete sentences.

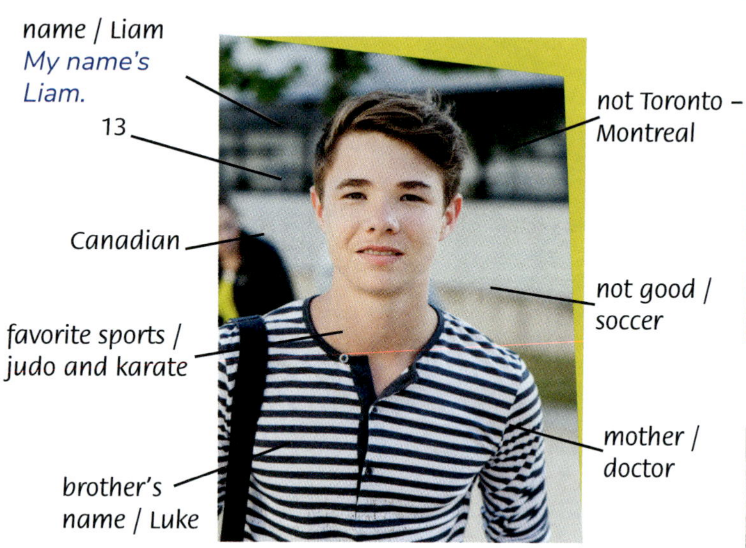

be: *Yes/No* questions

3 Order the words to make questions.

1 Jennifer Lawrence / Is / a singer ?
2 English class / Are / in an / we ?
3 you / Are / Brazilian ?
4 148 / the answer to 49 × 3 / Is ?
5 the Andes mountains / in / America / Are / South ?

4 Write short answers for the questions in exercise 3.

be: *Wh-* questions

5 Write questions about the underlined answers.

1 My name's <u>Christina</u>. *What's your name?*
2 I'm from <u>Athens</u>. _____
3 My mother's <u>45 years old</u>. _____
4 My favorite singer is <u>Zara Larsson</u>. _____
5 My favorite TV series is <u>Stranger Things</u>. _____

6 Write your own answers to the questions.

Possessive adjectives

7 Complete the sentences with a possessive adjective.

1 Me in *my* room.

2 Connor on _____ bike.

3 My sister on _____ first day at school.

4 We're moving to _____ new house!

5 My friend's cat with _____ favorite toy.

6 Mom and Dad on _____ wedding day.

Possessive 's and s'

8 **Rewrite two sentences as one sentence with possessive *'s* or *s'*.**

1. My brother has a computer. It's new.
   My brother's computer is new.
2. My friend has a sister. She's a student.
3. My parents have a car. It's blue.
4. Our neighbors have a dog. It's really cute.
5. My grandparents have a house. It's in Florida.
6. My dad has a brother. He lives in France.
7. I have two cousins. Their names are Tom and Louise.

have got

9 **Complete the description with *has/have got*.**

Paolo To: Lucas Friday

Hi! My name's Paolo and I'm from Italy. I **1** ________ a brother and a sister. My dad's name's Luigi. He's very short, and he **2** ________ black hair. My mom's Angela and she **3** ________ long brown hair. My dad **4** ________ any brothers or sisters, but my mom **5** ________ one brother. He's married to Sofia, and they **6** ________ two children, Enzo and Laura. We **7** ________ any pets. What about you? **8** ________ you ________ a big family?

Paolo

can for ability

10 **Look at the table. Complete the sentences with *can* or *can't*.**

 Monica	✔	✔	✔	✘	✘
 Damir	✘	✔	✘	✔	✔

1. Monica ________ speak French.
2. She ________ dance, but she ________ sing.
3. ________ Damir sing? Yes, he ________ , and he ________ also play the guitar.
4. ________ Monica play the guitar? No, she ________ .
5. Damir ________ speak French or dance.
6. Both Monica and Damir ________ ride a bike.

Unit 1

Simple present: affirmative and negative

1 Reinforcement **Change affirmative to negative and negative to affirmative.**

1. I take a shower before breakfast.
   I don't take a shower before breakfast.
2. She makes her bed in the morning.
3. He doesn't pack his bag in the evening.
4. We play basketball at school.
5. I do my homework after dinner.
6. They don't study German.
7. We don't go home together.

2 Reinforcement **Complete the table with the *he/she/it* form of the verbs.**

do go have listen play ~~speak~~ study teach clean try watch write

+ *-s*	+ *-es*	+ *-ies*	irregular
speaks			

3 Challenge **Continue the description of Sofia's day. Think carefully about all the changes you need to make.**

I wake up at seven o'clock and I have breakfast with my dad. After breakfast, I brush my hair and make my bed. I don't take a shower in the morning. I go to school by bus. I finish school at 3:30. I do my homework when I get home and I study for about an hour. Then I watch videos – I don't like TV. I go to bed at about 10 pm.

Sofia wakes up at seven o'clock and ...

Simple present: *Yes/No* questions

4 Reinforcement **Look at the colors and make sentences. Decide if the verb is *Do or Does*.**

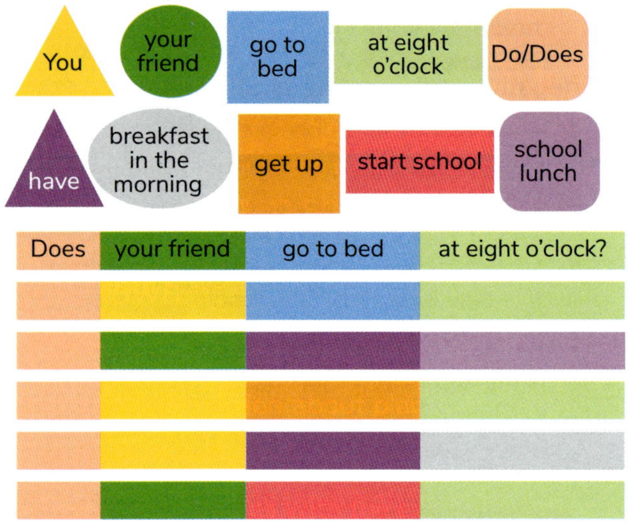

5 Reinforcement **Answer the questions with short answers, e.g. *Yes, I do./No, I don't.***

6 Challenge **Write a question and a short answer for each sentence.**

1 I study English.
Do you study English? ________ *Yes, I do.* ________
2 We have lunch at school.
________ ________
3 I don't like football.
________ ________
4 María lives in Las Rozas.
________ ________
5 My sister doesn't study physics.
________ ________

Object pronouns

7 Reinforcement **Match the subject pronouns with the object pronouns in the box.**

me him her it them us you

1 I 2 you 3 he 4 she
5 it 6 we 7 they

8 Challenge **Rewrite the sentences with pronouns.**

1 **My father** drives **a car** for work. *He drives it.*
2 **My aunt** loves **Italian food**.
3 **My cousins** help **their mom and dad** at home.
4 **Steven** watches TV with **Anna and me**.
5 **Anna and I** watch TV with **Steven**.

Unit 2

Adverbs of frequency

1 Reinforcement **Look at the diagrams and write the correct adverb of frequency.**

~~always~~ hardly ever never often sometimes usually

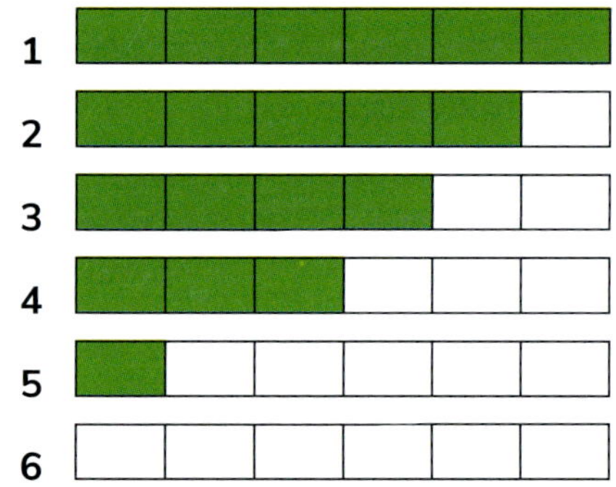

1 *always*
2 ________
3 ________
4 ________
5 ________
6 ________

2 Reinforcement **Rewrite the sentences with an adverb of frequency in the correct place so they are true for you.**

1 I go swimming on the weekend.
I sometimes go swimming on the weekend.
2 I go out with my friends on Saturday.
3 I watch videos on YouTube.
4 I do my homework on Sunday evening.
5 I'm hungry after playing sports.
6 I take photos to post on social media.

3 Challenge **Circle the correct option to complete the sentences.**

1 I (...) study a lot so I get good grades at school.
a never **b** hardly ever **c** always
2 My friend is (...) late for class, but she's usually on time.
a hardly ever **b** sometimes **c** never
3 My sister hates exercising so she (...) goes to the gym.
a always **b** never **c** sometimes
4 My brother (...) arrives home late because he goes to the library after school.
a often **b** hardly ever **c** never
5 I don't like eating in the school cafeteria so I (...) go home for lunch.
a never **b** hardly ever **c** usually
6 My grandparents live in another country so I (...) see them.
a always **b** hardly ever **c** often

4 Challenge **Write complete sentences with the adverb of frequency.**

1 It / be / hot here in the summer **(usually)**
2 My sister / go / skateboarding on Sundays **(often)**
3 You / have / the right books with you **(never)**
4 My parents / be / at home / on Saturday evenings **(hardly ever)**
5 My sister / do / yoga **(sometimes)**
6 I / get up late / on the weekend **(usually)**
7 We / watch online videos / we / watch TV **(always / never)**

Likes and dislikes

5 Reinforcement **Complete the sentences with the correct form of the verb.**

1 My cousin loves ________ badminton. **(play)**
2 I don't like ________ homework on Friday evening. **(do)**
3 My sister loves sleeping. She hates ________ early. **(get up)**
4 We love ________ computers in class. **(use)**
5 My dad likes ________ photos. He's really good at it. **(take)**
6 My brother hates ________ a TV series. **(watch)**
7 I don't mind ________ my bed or cleaning my room. **(make)**

6 Challenge **Write sentences about Sophie and Liam using the words in the box.**

collect do get up go listen
make take play practice use

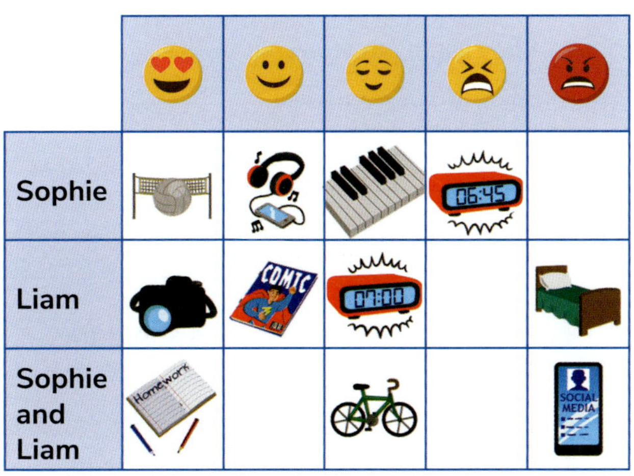

Sophie loves playing volleyball. She ...
Liam ...
They ...

Simple present: *Wh-* questions

7 Reinforcement **Circle the correct option.**

1 What **your favorite TV series is/is your favorite TV series**?
2 When **do you do/you do** your homework?
3 Why do **you have/have you** your math books? We have English now!
4 Where **does play your brother/does your brother play** field hockey?
5 Who **are those people/those people are** over there?
6 How many televisions **does your family/your family does** have?
7 How **do you get/do get you** to school? By bus or by bike?
8 What time **do your first class starts/does your first class start**?

8 Challenge **Read an interview with a teenage basketball player. Complete the questions to match his answers.**

Hi, Robert. Thanks for talking to me. Can you tell me about your typical day? **1** ________ get up?

At seven o'clock. I usually go for a run before breakfast. Then I go to school. I go to a special sports school.

Really? **2** ________ special?

It's special because it has a lot of sports facilities, like gyms and basketball courts.

3 ________ does it have?

It has six gyms!

Wow! And **4** ________ train?

I train in the evening, after school.

So **5** ________ hobbies?

My hobbies are listening to music and playing the guitar. Music really helps me.

How **6** ________ you ?

It helps me to relax.

OK, and finally, one more question. Who **7** ________ ?

My favorite basketball player is Giannis Antetokounmpo. He's awesome!

Thanks!

Unit 3

Present progressive

1 Reinforcement **Complete the table with the verbs in the box. Add the *-ing* form.**

~~clean~~ dance draw get go have
listen play practice read run sit
sleep take use watch wear write

+ -ing	~~e~~ + -ing	double consonant + -ing
cleaning		

2 Reinforcement **Write sentences in the present progressive.**

1

2

3

4

5

6
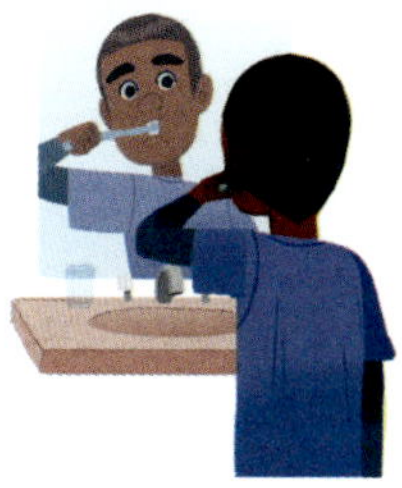

1 Tania / not / swim . She / run .
Tania isn't swimming. She's running.
2 Oliver / not / do / his homework . He / play / video games .
3 We / not / watch / TV . We / have / dinner .
4 My brother / not / sleep . He / listen / to music .
5 My friends / not / wear / dressy clothes . They / wear / casual clothes .
6 I / not / get dressed . I / brush / my teeth .

3 Reinforcement **Order the words to make questions.**

1 What / wearing / are / you / today ?
What are you wearing today?
2 shining / Is / the / sun ?
3 now / you / Are / having / lunch ?
4 talking / your / classmates / Are ?
5 your / What / is / teacher / doing ?

4 Challenge **Look at the picture and write sentences about what is happening.**

1 Mo / watch / TV
Mo isn't watching TV. He's playing video games.
2 He / sit / on the floor
____
3 He / wear / a hoodie
____
4 Becky / write / a letter
____
5 She / listen / to music
____
6 Josh and Ava / have / dinner
____
7 They / wear / their school uniform
____

5 Challenge **Write questions about the underlined information.**

1 I'm wearing <u>a shirt and jeans</u> today.
2 No, Jamie isn't <u>playing tennis</u> right now.
3 Sara is making <u>a video</u> for her class project.
4 They're studying <u>because they have a test</u>.
5 Yes, I am. I'm <u>doing my homework</u> right now.

Simple present and present progressive

6 Reinforcement **Circle the correct option. Use the time expressions to help you.**

1 Arjun usually (...) to school by bus.
 a go **b** goes **c** is going
2 Ryan and Megan aren't at home today. They (...) their grandparents.
 a usually visit **b** are visiting **c** is visiting
3 Matt (...) science, especially physics.
 a doesn't like **b** don't like **c** isn't liking
4 Alex can't talk to you right now. She (...) dinner.
 a have **b** has **c** is having
5 What time (...) ?
 a opens the library
 b does the library open
 c is opening the library
6 Miray (...) field hockey today. She's sick.
 a isn't playing **b** don't play
 c doesn't play
7 What (...) ? Is it a movie or a TV series?
 a do you watch **b** you are watching
 c are you watching

7 Challenge **Complete the email with the simple present or present progressive form of the verbs in parentheses.**

Adam To: Lucas Friday

Hi Lucas,

How are things? I **1** _________ **(stay)** with my cousins right now. They **2** _________ **(live)** in a small town. There isn't a lot to do here, so I **3** _________ **(write)** you this email. My uncle **4** _________ **(cook)** dinner and my aunt is at work – she always **5** _________ **(work)** late. My cousin Isla is in her room. I think she **6** _________ **(study)**. She usually **7** _________ **(spend)** a lot of time doing homework. My other cousin Jamie **8** _________ **(practice)** the guitar. He **9** _________ **(not like)** sports, and he hardly ever **10** _________ **(go)** out. It's very boring for me here!

What about you? What **11** _________ **(you/do)** right now? **12** _________ **(you/want)** to come and stay here with us for a few days? It would be great to see you! 🙂

Let me know.

Adam

Unit 4

Comparative and superlative adjectives

1 Reinforcement **Write the comparative and superlative forms of the adjectives.**

1 long
 longer – the longest
2 thin
 ____
3 important
 ____
4 trendy
 ____
5 bad
 ____
6 famous
 ____
7 expensive
 ____
8 quick
 ____

2 Reinforcement **Circle the correct option to complete the sentences.**

1 **The more/The most** famous soccer stadium in London is Wembley.
2 This is the **longer/longest** river in my country.
3 Math is more important **that/than** geography.
4 This is **most expensive/the most expensive** restaurant in my town.
5 It's not cold today. Wear a **thinner/thinnest** coat.
6 Claudia is the **trendier/trendiest** person I know.
7 The weather in the north of my country is **worst/worse** than in the south.
8 Trains are usually **quicker/quickest** than cars.

3 Challenge **Order the words to make sentences.**

1 biggest / Sydney / in Australia / is / the / city
 ____
2 than / My sandals / more / are / my boots / comfortable
 ____
3 more / math exams / history exams / than / are / difficult
 ____
4 student / best / Who / your class / is / the / in ?
 ____
5 in Mexico / She / famous / is / the most / one of / singers
 ____
6 in Turkey / is / The average temperature / higher / in Finland / than
 ____

4 Challenge **Complete the text with the comparative or superlative form of the adjectives in parentheses.**

Soccer and tennis are two of **1** ________ **(popular)** sports today and players like Eden Hazard and Gabriñe Muguruza are some of **2** ________ **(rich)** athletes, but who are **3** ________ **(fit)**: soccer or tennis players?

Players in both sports are **4** ________ **(strong)** now than in the past and soccer is definitely **5** ________ **(quick)**, but soccer games are usually **6** ________ **(short)** than tennis matches.

And which sport is **7** ________ **(good)** for people in general? A recent study from the University of Oxford says that people who play tennis are **8** ________ **(healthy)** than people who play soccer and live a **9** ________ **(long)** life.

Modal verbs of obligation, permission and prohibition

5 Reinforcement **Match questions 1–5 with answers a–e about camping in a national park.**

1 Can we take photos?
2 Can we camp anywhere in the park?
3 Can we cook on a fire?
4 Can we sit outside with other campers?
5 Can we walk anywhere we want?

a Yes, you can, but only in the campsites.
b No, you can't. You must stay on the paths.
c No, you can't. You can camp but only in the official campsites.
d Yes, you can. The park is a great place for photography.
e Yes, but you mustn't make any noise after midnight.

6 Reinforcement **Read answers a–e in exercise 5 and say if the underlined verbs describe permission, obligation or prohibition.**

a *Yes, you can, but only in the campsites.*
permission

7 Challenge **Read the school rules and circle the correct meaning.**

1 Students can bring their cell phones to school but at their own risk.
2 Students can't use cell phones during class.
3 All students must turn off their phones during class.
4 Students can use cell phones during breaks.
5 During a test, students must leave their phones at the front of the class.
6 On an official exam day, students must not bring their cell phones into the classroom.

1 a You decide to bring your phone to school or not.
b It's not OK to bring your phone to school.

2 a Do not use your phone when you are in class.
b Use your phone to check information on the internet during class.

3 a It's necessary to turn off your phone during class.
b It's not necessary to turn off your phone during class.

4 a Ask a teacher if you want to use your phone on a break.
b It's not a problem to use your phone on a break.

5 a During a test it's OK to have your phone on your desk.
b During a test your phone goes in a special place.

6 a Some days it's not possible to have your phone with you in class.
b Always have your phone with you in class.

8 Challenge **Read the rules and write four sentences with *can*, *can't*, *must* or *mustn't*. Use each word once.**

Unit 5

Countable and uncountable nouns

1 Reinforcement **Are the words in the box countable or uncountable?**

cheese guidebook library sunscreen sweater ~~team~~ toothpaste water

Countable: *team, ...*

Uncountable:

2 Reinforcement **Lisa is in the supermarket. She can't remember what food there is at home and writes a text to her brother Jake. Look at the photograph and write Jake's reply.**

I think we have three yogurts, some pasta and some eggs, a banana, butter and an onion, but we don't have any oil or any grapes. But I'm not sure. Can you check for me, Jake?

You're crazy, Lisa! Your list is so wrong! We have two yogurts ______

______

______

3 Challenge **Add *a/an* to the sentences. Be careful – some of the sentences are correct.**

1 We don't have *a* bike.
2 Do you like classical music?
3 Do you like Thai food?
4 Do you have minute?
5 My brother is looking for job.
6 Do you have time to help me?
7 Millie doesn't eat meat.
8 Cuba is island.

4 Challenge **Complete the dialogue.**

Hi. Do you have **1** ________ money? I'm hungry. I want to buy **2** ________ food.

Let's see. I have 5 dollars. We could go to Wok Land and get **3** ________ noodles.

Mmm, I don't want noodles. What about **4** ________ fries? Or we could get **5** ________ pizza to share?

That's a good idea. But we need **6** ________ more money. Do you have any?

Only **7** ________ dollar.

OK, fries then!

there is/are and *Is/Are there ...* ?

5 Reinforcement **Complete the description with *is* or *are*.**

I live right in the center of town. On my street there **1** ________ a department store and there **2** ________ lots of clothing stores. There **3** ________ several cafés and there **4** ________ a shopping center. Because of all the stores, there **5** ________ a lot of traffic. There **6** ________ always lots of cars on my street.

6 Reinforcement **Write questions with *Is there a/an...* ? or *Are there any...* ? Then answer the questions using the information in exercise 5.**

1 department store
Is there a department store? Yes, there is.
2 skate park
3 clothing stores
4 subway station
5 shopping center
6 music venues
7 library

7 Challenge **Order the words to make questions.**

1 museum / Is / in your town / there / a ?
2 on your street / Are / any / bus stops / there ?
3 many / in your / movie theaters / are / How / there / town ?
4 university / a / your town / Is / in / there ?
5 near where / castle / Is / you live / there a ?

8 Challenge **Answer the questions in exercise 7.**

Unit 6

Simple past: *be*

1 Reinforcement **Circle the correct option.**

1 We **wasn't/weren't** at school yesterday.
2 I **was/were** at home on Sunday afternoon.
3 You **was/were** late for class this morning. Why?
4 It **wasn't/weren't** cold last weekend.
5 There **was/were** a lot of people at the concert.
6 There **was/were** a thunderstorm last night.

2 Reinforcement **Order the words to make questions.**

1 were / Where / yesterday evening / you ?
2 your parents / Were / at home ?
3 they / Where / were ?
4 your brother / at home / Was ?
5 was / he / Where ?

3 Reinforcement **Complete the answers. Then match each answer with a question in exercise 2.**

a He ________ at a restaurant with friends.
b No, he ________ .
c They ________ at work.
d No, they ________ .
e I ________ at home, in my room.

4 Challenge **Complete the dialogue with the correct simple past form of *be*.**

1 Mom, where ________ you in this photo?

On vacation, in Nepal.

2 ________ Dad with you?

No, he **3** ________ . I **4** ________ with your grandparents.

5 ________ there a lot of animals in Nepal?

Yes, there **6** ________ rhinos, elephants and tigers!

Wow! **7** ________ it dangerous?

No, there **8** ________ a local guide with us, so we **9** ________ alone.

10 ________ it hot there?

Yes, very hot, but it **11** ________ amazing!

5 Challenge **Write questions about the picture using the past simple form of *be*.**

1 When / the School Fun Day ?
2 there / a field hockey game ?
3 there / any animals ?
4 Where / the photographer ?
5 there / any food ?
6 the students / in school uniform ?
7 Where / the teachers ?

6 Challenge **Answer the questions in exercise 5.**

Simple past of regular verbs: affirmative and negative

7 Reinforcement **Match verbs 1–4 with rules a–d. Then write the simple past form of the verbs.**

Verbs	Rules
1 finish, play	a + -d (...) (...)
2 live, dance	b ~~y~~ + -ied (...) (...)
3 stop, plan	c double consonant + -ed (...) (...)
4 study, try	d + -ed (...) (...)

8 Reinforcement **Correct the underlined information using words from the box.**

soccer Russia physics ~~millions of years ago~~ the Moon 1759

1 Dinosaurs lived 100 years ago.
Dinosaurs didn't live 100 years ago. They lived millions of years ago.
2 Stephen Hawking studied history.
3 David Beckham played basketball.
4 Neil Armstrong traveled to Mars.
5 The British Museum opened in 1959.
6 France organized the FIFA™ World Cup in 2018.

9 Challenge **Complete the article with the simple past of the regular and irregular verbs.**

Aaron and the Kakapo parrot

Aaron Friedman was in second grade at school when he first **1** _______ **(discover)** the bird. He **2** _______ **(go)** to a book fair and **3** _______ **(see)** a photo of the parrot in a book. At that time, there were only 122 of these birds in the world. Their natural habitat is the forests of New Zealand and Aaron lives in the US, but he **4** _______ **(not want)** them to disappear. He immediately **5** _______ **(decide)** to help.

Aaron **6** _______ **(start)** to save money and **7** _______ **(raise)** over $2,500 from family and friends to give to an organization. He also **8** _______ **(join)** a nature center and **9** _______ **(work)** as a volunteer at his local museum.

The number of birds is slowly growing, thanks to people like Aaron. He **10** _______ **(not wait)** for other people to solve the problem. 'It's my responsibility to try and help these birds,' he said.

Unit 7

Simple past of regular and irregular verbs

1 Reinforcement **Read the description. Write the simple past verbs in two lists: regular and irregular.**

During my summer vacation I decided to go and visit my cousin Daniel. I woke up early, had breakfast and took the 8:30 train. I arrived in Birmingham at about ten o'clock and Daniel met me at the station. First we went to buy some new sneakers. Then we visited this awesome gaming shop. We spent about an hour playing a new computer game. After that, we went to a skate park near Daniel's house, but it started raining so we went to his house for lunch. In the afternoon we watched a movie. I left at about 5 pm and got home at 7 pm. It was a great day!

Regular: *decided, …*

Irregular: *woke up, …*

2 Reinforcement **Write the base form of the verbs in exercise 1.**

decided – decide *woke up – wake up*

3 Reinforcement **Order the words to make questions. Then answer the questions using the information in exercise 1.**

1 or to / Did they / go to a game / the movies ?
2 the movie / was / What ?
3 it / did / When / start ?
4 sit / did / Where / they ?
5 have / to eat or drink / Did / they / anything ?
6 cost / did / How much / it ?

4 Challenge **Write the simple past form of the verbs in the box.**

be enjoy go have know leave meet see spend stay tell wake up

5 Challenge **Complete the sentences with the correct form of the verbs in exercise 4.**

1 I *met* Lucy for the first time at Jake's party. I ________ her before.
2 Samir ________ me that the movie was amazing, but when I saw it, I ________ it.
3 I ________ tired, so I ________ long at the party.
4 We ________ shopping this morning, but I ________ a lot of money.
5 I ________ Mom this morning. She ________ early for work.
6 I ________ at 5:30 am today because I ________ an exam this morning.

6 Challenge **Write questions using the verbs in parentheses to complete the dialogue.**

1 *What did you do* **(do)** on the weekend?
I went to Malaga to see my Uncle Pablo.
2 ______________ **(get)** there?
By train.
3 ______________ **(arrive)**?
At about 11:30 on Saturday morning.
4 ______________ **(stay)**?
At Pablo's house.
5 ______________ **(do)**?
On Saturday we went to the Picasso museum and on Sunday Pablo and I played tennis.
6 ______________ **(win)**?
No, he's much better than me!

Past time expressions

7 Reinforcement **Describe the time using the word *ago* and a word from the box.**

day hour month year

1 on Wednesday
two days ago
2 on Saturday
3 in 2019
4 last September
5 when I was 10
6 in February
7 at 6:00 am

8 Challenge **Complete the time expressions and write sentences that are true for you.**

1 I *learned to swim* when I was *five* years old.
2 I ____________ ____________ years ago.
3 I ____________ in ____________ .
4 I ____________ at the age of ____________ .
5 I ____________ ____________ months ago.
6 I ____________ last ____________ .

Unit 8

will for predictions

1 Reinforcement **Look at the pictures and complete the sentences with *will* or *won't* and a verb from the box.**

eat go have live travel use

In the future ...

1 people ________ on the Moon.

2 we ________ normal food.

3 students ________ Virtual Reality glasses at school.

4 every home ________ a robot.

5 we ________ by bus in cities.

6 people ________ to work.

2 Reinforcement **Use words from Box A and Box B to write five more questions about the future with *will*.**

Will you live in another country?

Box A	Box B
~~you live~~	the Earth
aliens visit	dinosaurs back to life
your country win	good English
scientists bring	possible
time travel be	~~in another country~~
you speak	the soccer World Cup

3 Reinforcement **Answer the questions in exercise 2 with short answers. Use your imagination!**

Yes, I will./No, I won't.

4 Challenge **Complete the article with *will* or *won't* and a verb in the box.**

be   not be   circle   cost   do   experience   not forget   open   not spend   travel

Will your next vacation be in space?

If you're looking for out-of-this-world accommodations, you **1** _________ happy to hear that a space hotel **2** _________ soon.

The hotel **3** _________ 200 miles (322 km) above the Earth, and it **4** _________ the Earth every 90 minutes. But it **5** _________ be cheap. It **6** _________ about 10 million dollars for 12 nights.

And guests in the hotel **7** _________ their time relaxing. They **8** _________ research and grow food too! But they **9** _________ zero gravity, and watch the sun rise 16 times a day. It'll be a vacation they **10** _________ for the rest of their lives!

5 Challenge **Write questions with *will* about the space hotel. Then answer the questions.**

1 When / the space hotel / open ?
2 How often / it / circle / the Earth ?
3 it / be / cheap ?
4 guests / relax / in this hotel ?
5 What / they / do ?
6 Why / it / be / an amazing experience ?

Future with *going to*

6 Reinforcement **Circle the correct option.**

1 A: What **you are/are you** going to do tonight?
B: I **going to/'m going to** play basketball.
2 A: Is your class going **have/to have** a party at the end of the term?
B: No, we **aren't/isn't** going to do anything.
3 A: When **Alex is/is Alex** going to do his project?
B: He **isn't/not** going to start it before Friday.
4 A: **Is going to Maria/Is Maria going to** study at college?
B: Yes, she's **going/going to** study engineering.

7 Challenge **Complete the email with *going to* and a verb from the box.**

not come   do   not have   go   spend   start   stay   study   work

Jed

Hi there!

Only two weeks until the end of the term! **1** (…) anything special to celebrate? We **2** (…) a party. Some friends and I **3** (…) for a pizza. Then I **4** (…) with my grandparents for two weeks. My sister **5** (…) with me because she has a part-time job. She **6** (…) in a café! What about you? Where **7** (…) your vacation? And your brother? I know this is his last year at school. **8** (…) college in October? What **9** (…) ?

Tell me your news. I'll write back straightaway.

Jed

Present progressive for future arrangements

8 Reinforcement **Write sentences in the present progressive.**

1 I / meet / my friend at the library at noon
I'm meeting my friend at the library at noon.
2 We / go / to Brazil in July
3 My dad / not work / on Saturday
4 What / you / do / on Sunday ?
5 We / have / a barbecue next weekend

9 Challenge **Complete the dialogue with the present progressive of the bold verbs.**

Hugo: **1** _________ your cousin _________ **(come)** to stay with you again this summer?

Jade: Yes, she is. In fact, she **2** _________ **(arrive)** today. We **3** _________ **(meet)** her at the bus station at eleven.

Hugo: Great! So, **4** _________ you _________ **(go)** anywhere later?

Jade: No, we **5** _________ **(have)** dinner at home. I think she'll be tired, but Mom **6** _____ **(get)** tickets for us to go on a bus tour on Sunday. Do you want to come?

Hugo: I'd love to! How long **7** _________ she _____ **(stay)** ?

Jade: Just five days. She **8** _________ **(travel)** back to New York next Friday.

Pronunciation

Unit 1
Silent letters

Some words in English have silent letters: we write the letter but we do not say it.

1 59 **Listen to the words. Which letters are not pronounced?**

1 history
2 design
3 technology
4 literature
5 chemistry
6 science

2 Find the silent letters in the words.

1 separate
2 camera
3 chocolate
4 cousin
5 cupboard
6 daughter
7 guitar
8 interesting
9 favorite
10 white

3 60 **Listen and check. Repeat the words in exercise 2.**

Unit 2
do you /djʊ/

1 61 **Listen to the questions. Underline the stressed words.**

1 What sport do you like?
2 When do you play?
3 Where do you play?
4 Who do you play with?
5 Why do you like this sport?

Pronunciation of *do you*

When the words *do you* aren't stressed in a question, we often pronounce them /djʊ/.

2 62 **Listen and repeat /djʊ/.**

3 Listen again and repeat the questions in exercise 1.

Unit 3
/n/ and /ŋ/

1 63 **Listen and repeat the words with /n/.**

sneakers sandals clean design

2 64 **Listen and repeat the words with /ŋ/.**

English think practicing singer

3 65 **Listen to the words. Do you hear a or b?**

1 **a** thin **b** thing
2 **a** call in **b** calling
3 **a** win **b** wing
4 **a** go in **b** going

4 66 **Listen and repeat the tongue-twisters.**

1 Lynne is wearing thin pink leggings.
2 I'm singing and Finn is playing the violin.

Unit 4
can

/kæn/ or /kən/?

In questions and affirmative sentences, *can* is not stressed, so we say /kən/.

In short answers, we say /kæn/.

1 67 **Listen to the two pronunciations of *can*.**

1 /kæn/ 2 /kən/

2 Look at the dialogue. How do you say *can* in each case, /kən/ or /kæn/?

A: **1** Can I go shopping this afternoon?
B: Yes, you **2** can. You **3** can get some new sneakers.
A: **4** Can Ellen come with me?
B: Yes, she **5** can. You **6** can go to that new fast-food restaurant.

3 68 **Listen and check your answers in exercise 2. Practice the dialogue in pairs.**

Unit 5

/i/ and /ɪ/

1 69 **Listen and repeat the words with a long *i* sound /i/.**

beef cheese peas read teach we

2 70 **Listen and repeat the words with a short *i* sound /ɪ/.**

bit thin gym milk physics wind

3 **Find the /i/ and /ɪ/ sounds in the sentence.**

Six teams are swimming in the freezing sea.

4 71 **Listen to the words. Is the sound short or long?**

1 eat
2 it
3 skin
4 minute
5 sheep
6 liquid

Unit 6

Simple past endings /d/ /t/ /ɪd/

Pronouncing *-ed*

There are three pronunciations of *-ed* endings: /d/ /t/ and /ɪd/.

1 72 **Listen to the pronunciation of the verbs in the table.**

/d/	/t/	/ɪd/
played	*watched*	*visited*

2 73 **Copy the table in exercise 1. Listen and add the verbs in the box.**

finished decided helped listened needed received started stopped traveled

3 **What letters come before /ɪd/?**

4 74 **Listen and repeat the verbs in the table.**

5 75 **Listen and repeat the sentences.**

1 I watched a movie last night.
2 I played soccer on Saturday.
3 We visited London last year.
4 We traveled by train.
5 I helped my mom yesterday.

Unit 7

Schwa /ə/

Letters in unstressed syllables

We pronounce some letters in unstressed syllables as /ə/. We call this sound 'schwa'.

1 76 **Listen and repeat the sound /ə/.**

2 77 **Listen to the jobs. Where do you hear /ə/?**

1 singer
2 lawyer
3 doctor
4 accountant
5 receptionist
6 photographer

3 **Listen again and repeat the words.**

4 78 **Listen to the sentences. How many times do you hear /ə/ in each sentence?**

1 She's a lawyer.
2 He's a good doctor.
3 My brother's an actor.
4 I'd like to be a teacher.

Unit 8

will

Contracted form

We usually use *will* in the contracted form *'ll*.

1 79 **Listen and repeat the contractions.**

I'll you'll he'll she'll we'll they'll

2 80 **Listen to the contractions in complete sentences and repeat.**

1 I'll see you at 8 o'clock.
2 She'll be here in 10 minutes.

3 81 **Listen. Do you hear a or b?**

1 **a** I go by bus. **b** I'll go by bus.
2 **a** We watch TV. **b** We'll watch TV.
3 **a** They play sports. **b** They'll play sports.
4 **a** You live in the city. **b** You'll live in the city.
5 **a** I speak English. **b** I'll speak English.

4 **Listen to the answers again and repeat.**

5 **Work in pairs. Say a sentence in exercise 3. Can your partner tell which you are saying (a or b)?**

Project planner

Unit 1 Graphic organizer

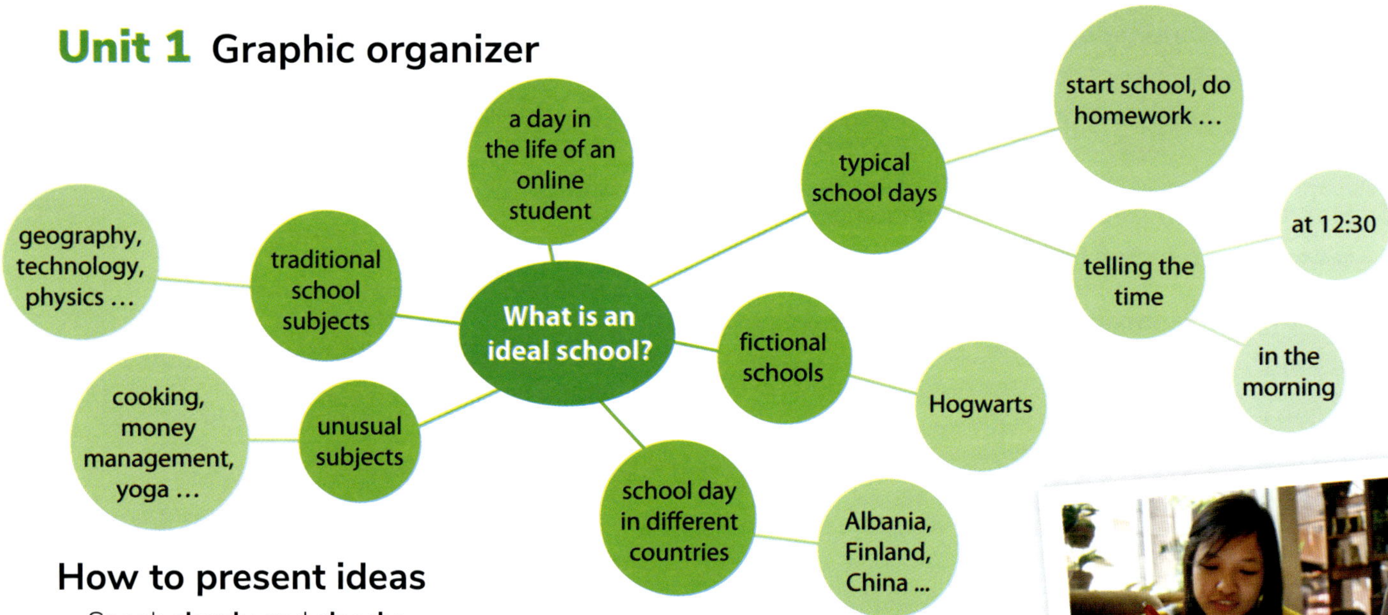

How to present ideas

- Speak **slowly** and **clearly**.
- **Don't read!**
- Look at **your classmates** when you speak.
- **Pause** after each sentence. Give your classmates time to understand.
- Point to your **visual material** to help your classmates understand.

Unit 2 Graphic organizer

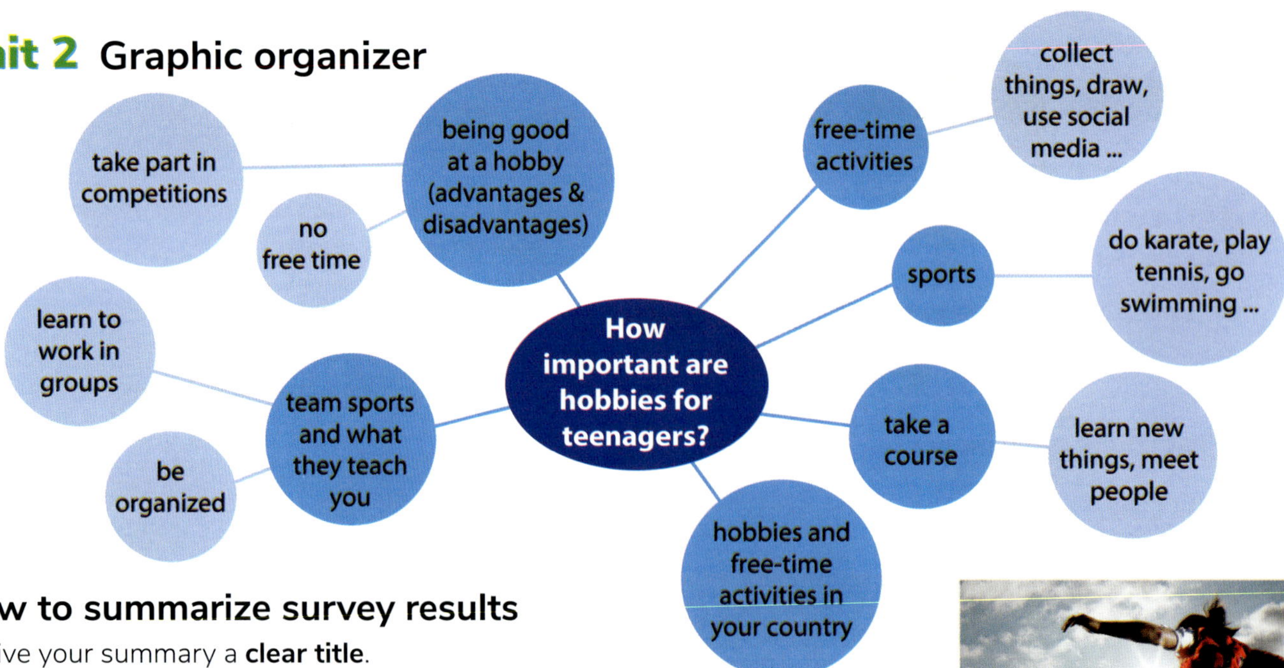

How to summarize survey results

- Give your summary a **clear title**.
- Organize your summary in **clear paragraphs**.
- Use **appropriate language** (*Most people … People always/usually/sometimes …*)
- **Be specific** about numbers (*Six people … Only four people …*)
- Give **examples** (*The most popular … is …*)

Unit 3 Graphic organizer

How to make an attractive mini-book

- Include a **title**.
- Use **pictures**: photos, maps, drawings, diagrams, etc.
- Use different **colors**.
- Write **clearly**.
- Have **short paragraphs**.
- Vary the **layout** of the pages.

Unit 4 Graphic organizer

How to make a video

- Record your video in a **light place**.
- Make sure that there isn't a lot of extra **noise**.
- **Stand still** when you speak.
- Look at the camera – and **smile**!
- Speak **loudly** and **clearly**.
- **Pause** between different sections.

Unit 5 Graphic organizer

How to present visual information

- Make sure people can see. **Don't block the visual** with your body.
- **Start with a general introduction** of your visual. **Then explain the details**.
- Use a **pointer or pen** to indicate what you are talking about.
- **Give people time** to see where you are pointing before you speak.

Unit 6 Graphic organizer

How to give a presentation about a poster

- Organize your presentation into **clear sections**.
- Plan a phrase to **introduce each section** (*Now let's look at its habitat.*).
- **Decide** who's saying each part.
- **Take your time**: it isn't a problem to pause. People need time to listen and understand.

Unit 7 Graphic organizer

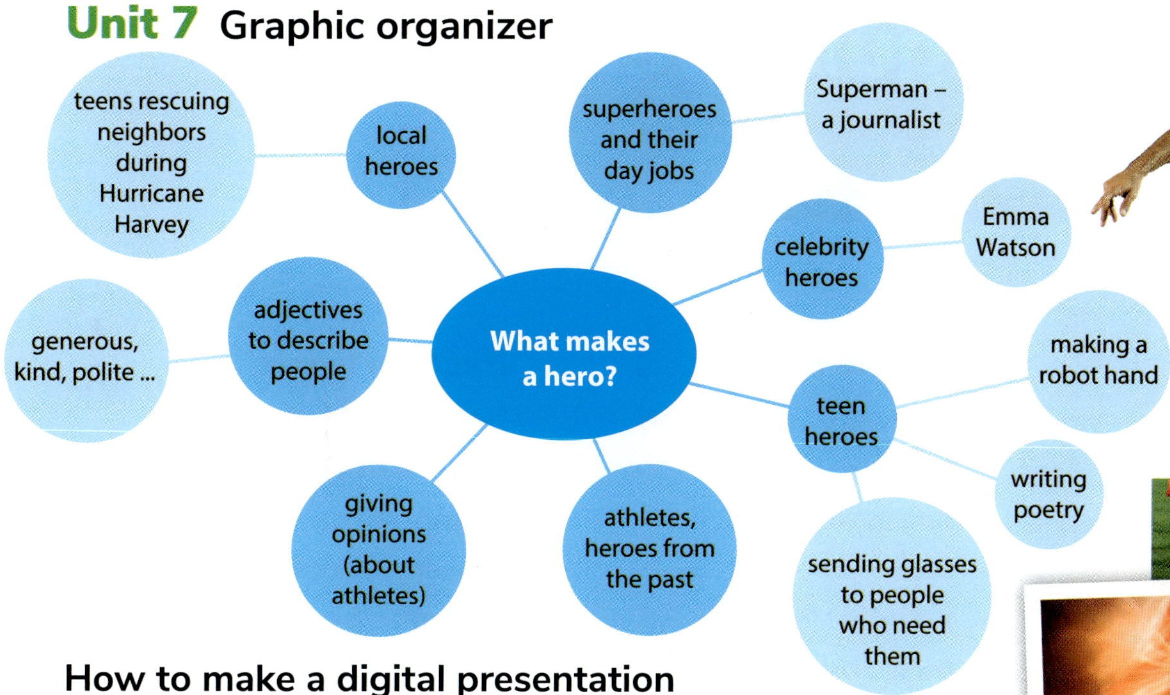

How to make a digital presentation

- Start with a **picture** and/or **questions** to get people interested.
- Use **titles** on each page.
- Have a **picture** on each slide.
- Don't write all the information that you want to say. Have **simple facts**.
- Prepare what you want to say with each slide. Write **notes** that can help you to remember.
- **Practice** what you want to say.

Unit 8 Graphic organizer

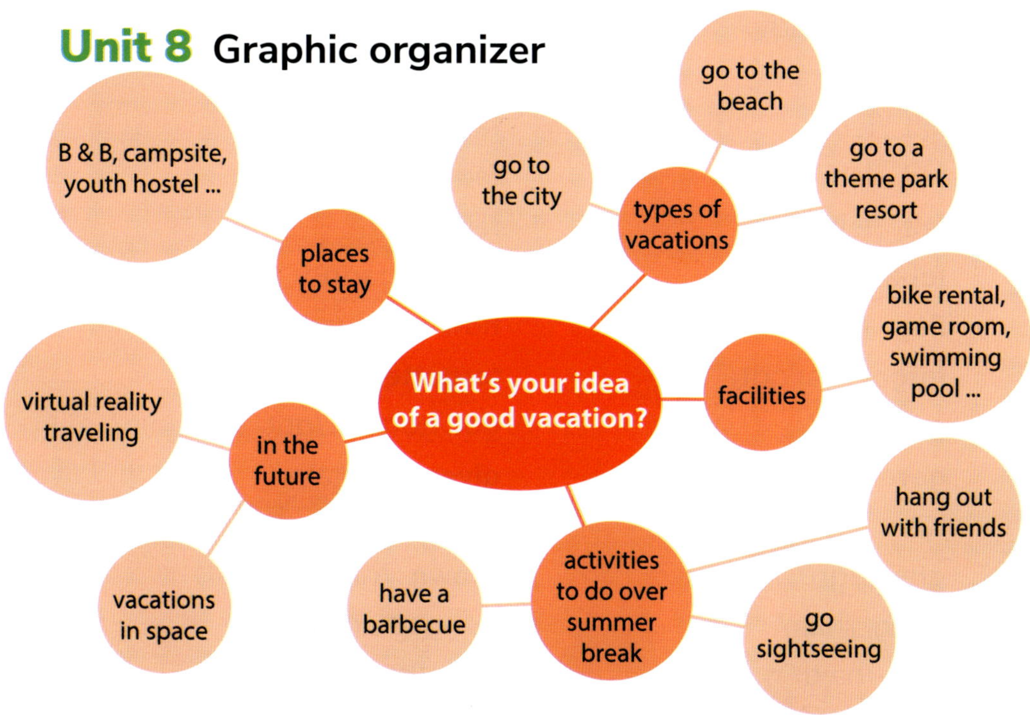

How to indicate the steps of your presentation

- Start with a **clear introduction** to explain what your presentation is about (*I'm going to talk about ...*)
- Use words like ***first***, **after that** and ***finally*** so listeners know you're moving to a new point.
- Give an opportunity for **listeners to ask questions**.
- At the end, **thank people for listening**.

Irregular verbs

Base form	Simple past	Past participle
be /bi/	**was/were** /wɑz/ /wɜr/	**been** /bɪn/
become /bɪˈkʌm/	**became** /bɪˈkeɪm/	**become** /bɪˈkʌm/
begin /bɪˈɡɪn/	**began** /bɪˈɡæn/	**begun** /bɪˈɡʌn/
break /breɪk/	**broke** /broʊk/	**broken** /ˈbroʊkən/
bring /brɪŋ/	**brought** /brɔt/	**brought** /brɔt/
build /bɪld/	**built** /bɪlt/	**built** /bɪlt/
buy /baɪ/	**bought** /bɔt/	**bought** /bɔt/
catch /kætʃ/	**caught** /kɔt/	**caught** /kɔt/
choose /tʃuz/	**chose** /tʃoʊz/	**chosen** /ˈtʃoʊz(ə)n/
come /kʌm/	**came** /keɪm/	**come** /kʌm/
cut /kʌt/	**cut** /kʌt/	**cut** /kʌt/
do /du/	**did** /dɪd/	**done** /dʌn/
drink /drɪŋk/	**drank** /dræŋk/	**drunk** /drʌŋk/
drive /draɪv/	**drove** /droʊv/	**driven** /ˈdrɪv(ə)n/
eat /it/	**ate** /eɪt/	**eaten** /ˈit(ə)n/
fall /fɔl/	**fell** /fel/	**fallen** /ˈfɔlən/
feed /fid/	**fed** /fed/	**fed** /fed/
feel /fil/	**felt** /felt/	**felt** /felt/
find /faɪnd/	**found** /faʊnd/	**found** /faʊnd/
fly /flaɪ/	**flew** /flu/	**flown** /floʊn/
forget /fərˈget/	**forgot** /fərˈgɑt/	**forgotten** /fərˈgɑt(ə)n/
get /get/	**got** /gɑt/	**got, gotten** /gɑt/ /ˈgɑt(ə)n/
give /gɪv/	**gave** /geɪv/	**given** /ˈgɪv(ə)n/
go /goʊ/	**went** /went/	**gone** /gɑn/
grow /groʊ/	**grew** /gru/	**grown** /groʊn/
hang /hæŋ/	**hung** /hʌŋ/	**hung** /hʌŋ/
have /hæv/	**had** /hæd/	**had** /hæd/
hear /hɪr/	**heard** /hɜrd/	**heard** /hɜrd/
hit /hɪt/	**hit** /hɪt/	**hit** /hɪt/

Base form	Simple past	Past participle
keep /kip/	**kept** /kept/	**kept** /kept/
know /noʊ/	**knew** /nu/	**known** /noʊn/
lay /leɪ/	**laid** /leɪd/	**laid** /leɪd/
leave /liv/	**left** /left/	**left** /left/
let /let/	**let** /let/	**let** /let/
lose /luz/	**lost** /lɑst/	**lost** /lɑst/
make /meɪk/	**made** /meɪd/	**made** /meɪd/
meet /mit/	**met** /met/	**met** /met/
pay /peɪ/	**paid** /peɪd/	**paid** /peɪd/
put /pʊt/	**put** /pʊt/	**put** /pʊt/
read /rid/	**read** /red/	**read** /red/
ride /raɪd/	**rode** /roʊd/	**ridden** /'rɪd(ə)n/
ring /rɪŋ/	**rang** /ræŋ/	**rung** /rʌŋ/
run /rʌn/	**ran** /ræn/	**run** /rʌn/
say /seɪ/	**said** /sed/	**said** /sed/
see /si/	**saw** /sɔ/	**seen** /sin/
sell /sel/	**sold** /soʊld/	**sold** /soʊld/
send /send/	**sent** /sent/	**sent** /sent/
shine /ʃaɪn/	**shone** /ʃoʊn/	**shone** /ʃoʊn/
sing /sɪŋ/	**sang** /sæŋ/	**sung** /sʌŋ/
sit /sɪt/	**sat** /sæt/	**sat** /sæt/
sleep /slip/	**slept** /slept/	**slept** /slept/
speak /spik/	**spoke** /spoʊk/	**spoken** /'spoʊkən/
spend /spend/	**spent** /spent/	**spent** /spent/
sweep /swip/	**swept** /swept/	**swept** /swept/
swim /swɪm/	**swam** /swæm/	**swum** /swʌm/
take /teɪk/	**took** /tʊk/	**taken** /'teɪkən/
teach /titʃ/	**taught** /tɔt/	**taught** /tɔt/
tell /tel/	**told** /toʊld/	**told** /toʊld/
think /θɪŋk/	**thought** /θɔt/	**thought** /θɔt/
throw /θroʊ/	**threw** /θru/	**thrown** /θroʊn/
understand /ˌʌndər'stænd/	**understood** /ˌʌndər'stʊd/	**understood** /ˌʌndər'stʊd/
wake /weɪk/	**woke** /woʊk/	**woken** /'woʊkən/
win /wɪn/	**won** /wʌn/	**won** /wʌn/
write /raɪt/	**wrote** /roʊt/	**written** /'rɪt(ə)n/

Macmillan Education Limited
4 Crinan Street
London N1 9XW

Companies and representatives throughout the world

Get Involved! American Edition Level 1 Student's Book ISBN 978-1-380-03308-6
Get Involved! American Edition Level 1 Student's Book with Student's App and Digital Student's Book ISBN 978-1-380-07215-3

First published 2022

Original design by Designers Educational Ltd and emc design ltd
Page make-up by Wild Apple Design Ltd and Composure
Illustrated by Alexandra Barboza (Lemonade Illustration Agency) pp. 89, 120(l); Esther Cuadrado (Beehive Illustration) pp. 40, 124; Daniela Geremia (Beehive Illustration) pp. 13, 64, 114; David Hurtado (Beehive Illustration) pp. 48, 49, 65, 71; Tamara Joubert (Beehive Illustration) pp. 56, 119, 123; Peter Lubach (Beehive Illustration) p. 7; Camille Medina (Beehive Illustration) p. 17; Jim Peacock (Beehive Illustration) pp. 9, 120(r), 126; Martin Sanders (Beehive Illustration) p. 67; Kate Sheppard (Beehive Illustration) pp. 19, 52
Cover design by Designers Educational Ltd
Cover photographs by Getty Images/Tony Anderson (bl), Alamy/Serhii Bobyk (br), Getty Images/Maskot (tr,cm), Getty Images/Pollyana Ventura (tl)
Picture research by Catherine Dunn
Cover picture research by Penelope Bowden, Proudfoot Pictures

Authors' acknowledgements
Gill would like to thank her friends from International House, Barcelona.
Kate would like to thank all her colleagues and friends at International House, Madrid.

The publishers would like to thank Nancy Contreras Guerrero; Luciana Gugliada S.; Nuria Julieta Holguin Añoveros, Colegio Benavente; Edith Dolores Islas Cabrera, Colegio Hispano Americano; Silvana Flores López, Instituto D'Amicis, S.C.; Monica Muñoz Castanón; Jaqueline Suzanne Torres Contreras.

The authors and publishers would like to thank the following for permission to reproduce their photographs:
Airbus/p. 100(cr); **From the Alamy Stock Photo collection**: leonello calvetti p. 74(tr), CBP Photo p. 87(t), Ian Dagnall p. 68(tl), Danita Delimont p. 12(m), Geisler-Fotopress p. 15(bl), Richard Green p. 39(g), Graham Jepson p. 24(tr), Natalia Klenova p. 37(e), Ruslan Kudrin p. 41(d), Marisa Lia p. 41(b), Fco Javier Rivas Martín p. 39(f), Mooodboard p. 25(m), PA Images p. 77(bl), Malcolm Park p. 39(e), Pictoral Press p. 38(br), Helene Rogers p. 36(sandals), Mark Shahaf p. 66(tr), Wdnet Studio p. 130(cr), Hugh Threlfall p. 41(a), TitoOnz p. 48(tr), Xinhua p. 87(bl), ZUMA Press, Inc. p. 52(tr); **Antonio Zazueta Olmos**/p. 89(2); **AP Images**/Associated Press p. 28(mr); **BBC Studios Distribution LTD.**/pp. 3(tl), 37 (br), 85 (br); **Betjeman Poetry Prize**/p. 89(6); **Comicon**/Anthony Byrne pp. 11(4), 38(b), 39(d); **DLA**/pp. 13(br), 61(br); **g4g**/p. 75(tr); **Getty Images**/p. 25(tl), 1001nights p. 47(tl, tr), adamkaz p. 112(tr), AFP Contributor p. 87(br), Anadolu Agency pp. 11(8), 16(tr), AndreyPopov p. 32(tl), Ar Duche Misfa'l p. 104(6), Artisteer p. 89(4), BarcroftMedia p. 13(m), Thomas Barwick pp. 24(m), 130(br), Believe_In_Me p. 41(e), Bhofack2 pp. 60(3), 115(tr), Boston Globe p. 80(tl), David Cabrera pp. 68(t), 132(tl), Kryissa Campos p. 72(cl), ManikChauhan p. 63(a), RazvanChisu pp. 96(2), 133(br), Cmcderm 1 pp. 10(4), 25(1), Donaldson Collection p. 95(tl), Dean Conger pp. 11(3), 50(b), 51(bl), 131(b), CustomDesigner pp. 53(d), 131(br), d3sign p. 3(m), daitoZen p. 60(1), Danicek p. 53(e), Dado Daniela p. 114(t), Donna Day p. 79(goat), Steve Debenport pp. 12(tr), 34(t), Dendong p. 41(f), Elitsia Deykova p. 99(tl), DGLimages p. 8(c), Domin_domin p. 53(f), Jerry Driendl pp. 101(1), 133(bcr), Duci86 p. 90(tr), Dulezidar p. 61(7), Sam Edwards pp. 25(2), 41(tr), Envirionmantic p. 63(d), Don Farrall p. 73(bee), FatCamera p. 8(b), Fotografo p. 54(tr), FS-Stock p. 29(karate), Fuse p. 101(5), G15702993 p. 60(2), Gbh007 p. 101(3), Aurelian Gogonea p. 73(4), Dinoco Greco p. 14(b), Green_Leaf p. 41(c), Judith Haeusler p. 101(4), Sean M. Haffey p. 27(m), Halfpoint p. 10(10), Hello World p. 36(c), Hero Images pp. 14(i), 18(m), 25(5, 6), 104(tl), 108(f), 116(2), Miodrag Ignjatovic p. 23(c), Itsabreeze Photography p. 73(3), Ivanastar p. 89(3), jewhyte p. 107(b), Zhou Jiang p. 104(t), Johnner Images p. 14(c), Hugh Johnston p. 79(horse), I. Jonsson p. 41(g), Beverley Joubert p. 99(tr), Simala Kama p. 108(g), Kanawa_Studio p. 15(tl), Keeweeboy p. 10(7), Dorling Kindersley p. 89(5), Kirby p. 92(tr), Victor Kitaykin p. 53(k), Mitchell Krog p. 75(tr), Reinhard Krull p. 29(field hockey), Chalermphon Kumchai p. 17(tl), Minoru Kuriyama p. 97(6), Hein L p. 117(bike), Mark Leech p. 122(tll), Sandra Leidholdt p. 72(cr), Lenta p. 37(g), Ljupco p. 37(h), Lonely Planet Images p. 107(tr), Catherine MacBride p. 42(m), MachineHeadz p. 13(tl), Peeranon Mahanil p. 84(airplane), Malerapaso p. 53(b), Turgay Malikili p. 104(5), Manakin p. 53(c), Adriana Marteva p. 61(5), martinedoucet p. 8(Australia), mawielobob p. 43(dress), MediaProduction p. 41(h), Jasmin Merdan p. 117(boy), Donald Miralle pp. 2(bl), 11(5), 27(t), Monticello p. 53(a), Morsa Images p. 117(girl), NASA p. 95(cr), Cristian Negroni p. 44(tl), Francoise Nel p. 122(tlr), Newscast p. 109(bl), Thorsten Nilson p. 83(tl), Bet Noire p. 112(news update), Thomas Northcut p. 32(tr), Olivia Bell Photography p. 36(a), Gary Ombler p. 73(rhino), SvetaOrlova p. 29(aerobics), Daniel Osterkamp p. 72(t), Pacific Press p. 88(cr), Parrotstarr p. 73(parrot), LauriPatterson p. 63(b), Simon Pinolla p. 10(8), Pixeliebe p. 28(bl), Poerofforever p. 29(skates), Witthaya Prasongsin p. 85(camera), Sarote Pruksachat p. 96(3), Prapass Pulsub p. 117(guitar), David Ramos pp. 25(4), 91(trr), 133(tr), LowellRichards p. 83(cr), Elles Rijsdikj p. 117(microphone), Riou p. 108(i), Rohappy p. 44(t), Lauri Rotko p. 59(cr), Roundhill p. 10(1), Chris Ryan p. 103(trm), Pete Saloutos p. 36(d), Carsten Schanter p. 99(br), Sharoncudworth p. 112(teen talk), Sidekick p. 23(b), Sitikka p. 59(tl), Tim Snell p. 65(m), Solstock pp. 12(c), 20(tl), 130(tr), Staff p. 88(bl), Bob Stevens pp. 14(e), 25(3), Stock Colours p. 55(tr), James Stone J p. 99(bl), Marie Stone p. 112(natural science), Paul Sutherland p. 79(chicken), Monica and Michael Sweet pp. 72(tr), 115(br), Stephen Swintek p. 101(6), Cordier Sylvain p. 108(a), szeyuen p. 8(d), Chris Danielle Tabangay p. 63(c), Burcu Atalay Tankut p. 60(4), Tetra Images p. 14(d, j), theasis p. 107(cr), TimeStopper p. 85(technology), Tirc83 p. 102(cr), Victor Tyakht pp. 11(2), 75(bl), p. ValuaVitaly p. 37(f), Klaus Vedfelt p. 23(d), Richard Villalon p. 53(g), Visionhaus p. 91(trl), Theo Wargo/Staff p. 97(br), Westend61 pp. 15(tr), 30(cr, cl), 103(trl), 112(good cooking), 116(cl), Kim Westerskov p. 95(t), Whitewish p. 64(m), Wwing p. 53(h), Xingmin07 p. 12(background), Poh Kim Yeoh pp. 36(outfit), 37(i); **Macmillan Education Limited**/pp. 3(fish), 3(tr), 12(bl), 19(tl), 22(m), 24(bl), 31(tl), 34(cl), 36(bl), 43(tl), 46(m), 48(bl), 49(br), 55(tl), 58(m), 60(bl), 62(bl), 64(grapes), 67(tl), 70(tr), 72(bl), 73(br), 77(b), 79(tl), 82(m), 84(bl), 86(b), 91(tl), 94(cl), 96(bl), 97(cr), 103(tl), 106(cl), 113(tr), Alamy pp. 43(jacket), 99(br), 108(c), 116(3), Bananastock pp. 53(tl), 103(trr), Comstock pp. 3(cheese), 64(cheese), Corbis pp. 25(br), 26(br), Digital Vision pp. 73(6), 78(tr), Getty Images pp. 3(grapes, milk, peas), 6(br), 10(3, 9), 14(a, h), 23(a), 53(i, j), 56, 61(6), 63(e), 64(fish, milk, peas), 68(tr), 73(2), 73(5), 76 (boy, fossil, girl1, girl2), 78(br), 84(briefcase, news), 97(4, 5, 7), 99(cl), 104(tr), 107(tl), 108(b, e), 109(br), 112(future world, sports live, tech news, travel tips), 116(5, 6), 117(br), 125(cl), 127(tl), 132(cr), Image Source p. 10(5, 6), Istock p. 108(d), iStockphoto pp. 43(shoes), 73(1), 115(shoes),116(1, 4), Johner Images p. 17(tr), PhotoDisc pp. 96(1), 108(h), 117(ballet shoes), PhotoDisc/Getty Images p. 85(beakers), Stockbyte p. 6(Ireland), Superstock pp. 6(Australia. Brazil, Japan, Nigeria, Turkey), 62(a, b, c, d, e) 117(france); **NASA**/p. 95(tr); **Shutterstock.com**/p. 95(cr), Aratehortua p. 104(1), Roberta Basile pp. 39(c), 131(tr), Boris15 p. 75(br), Carboxylase p. 104(2), Amos Chapple p. 51(tl, tr), ric Charbonneau p. 39(b), Cosmic_Design p. 104(3), ESB Professional p. 80(tr), Peter Hermes Furian p. 92(background), gresei pp. 43(jeans), 115(jeans), Andrea Izzotti p. 73(dolphin), Jerry1259 p. 2(m), Julia Kaysa p. 10(2), Kobal p. 84(superman), Kobal/Columbia p. 85(spiderman), Kobal/Marvel/Disney pp. 2(tl), 85(shuri), Kobal/Marvel Enterprises p. 85(iron man), Mario Laporta p. 39(a), Monkey Business Images p. 14(f,g), Moviestore pp. 11(1), 84(batman, captain marvel), 133(tcr), Evgeniya Porechenskaya pp. 43(hoodie), 115(hoodie), Susan Schmitz p. 73(snake), Vasyl Shulga p. 115(cl), Charles Sykes pp. 11(7), 77(br), 132(br), VectorsMarket p. 104(4), Roger-Viollet p. 92(trb), wavebreakmedia p. 31(tr), xpixel p. 31(tm); **Unlimited Tomorrow**/p. 89(1).

Video footage and stills supplied by:
BBC Studios Distribution Ltd pp. 3, 37, 85; Digeo Productions pp. 24, 46, 49, 73, 97; DLA pp. 13, 61; MTJ pp. 3, 19, 31, 43, 55, 67, 79, 91, 103; Maia Films pp. 3, 22, 34, 58, 70, 82, 94, 106

Additional sources:
Baldwin, S. (04/10/2014) 'The future of travel: Gareth Williams, Skyscanner CEO predicts', Skyscanner.net

Printed and bound in Uruguay

2024
30